Elite • 244

Soldiers of Fortune

Mercenaries & Military Adventurers 1960–2020

ANTHONY ROGERS

ILLUSTRATED BY PETER DENNIS
Series editors Martin Windrow & Nick Reynolds

OSPREY PUBLISHING
Bloomsbury Publishing Plc

Kemp House, Chawley Park, Cumnor Hill, Oxford OX2 9PH, UK
29 Earlsfort Terrace, Dublin 2, Ireland
1385 Broadway, 5th Floor, New York, NY 10018, USA
Email: info@ospreypublishing.com
www.ospreypublishing.com

OSPREY is a trademark of Osprey Publishing Ltd

First published in Great Britain in 2022

A catalogue record for this book is available from the British Library.

Print ISBN: 978 1 4728 4801 7
ePub : 978 1 4728 4796 6
ePDF: 978 1 4728 4797 3
XML: 978 1 4728 4795 9

Editor: Martin Windrow
Index by Zoe Ross
Typeset by PDQ Digital Media Solutions, Bungay, UK
Printed and bound in India by Replika Press Private Ltd.

22 23 24 25 26   10 9 8 7 6 5 4 3 2

ACKNOWLEDGEMENTS
In addition to those whose photographs are individually credited, and
others who prefer to remain anonymous, the author also wishes to thank
the following for their contributions:
Derek Andrews, Pat Armstrong, Alan Boydell, Charlie Brown, Fraser Brown,
Jon Caffin, Cliffy Clifford, Royce de Melo, Dusty Duncan, Neall Ellis, Mark
Galeotti, Ken Gaudet, Gilly Gillmore, Barry Gribbin, Shaun Gullan, Henri
Lepetit, Pieter Nortje, Jonathan Pittaway (who kindly liaised with a number
of individuals and associations), Lang Price, Rob Riddell, Dean Shelley,
Glenn Thomas, and Al J. Venter.

ARTIST'S NOTE
Readers may care to note that the original paintings from which the colour
plates in this book were prepared are available for private sale. All
reproduction copyright whatsoever is retained by the publishers. All
enquiries should be addressed to:

Peter Dennis, 'Fieldhead', The Park, Mansfield, Nottinghamshire NG18 2AT, UK

The publishers regret that they can enter into no correspondence upon this
matter.

FRONT COVER PHOTO Volunteers serving with Support Commando, 1st
Battalion, Rhodesian Light Infantry, c. 1978. From left to right: Barry Gribbin
(USA), Chris Rogers (New Zealand), Ian Traynor (UK), and Martin Overbeck
(New Zealand). (Private collection)

Acronyms & abbreviations used in this text

ADFL	Democratic Forces for Liberation of Congo	GUNT	Transitional Government of National Unity (in Chad)	PSU	Police Support Unit (Rhodesian)
ANC	Congolese National Army, or African National Congress (S. Africa)	GSG	Gurkha Security Guards Ltd	RAR	Rhodesian African Rifles
		HOS	Croatian Defence Forces (militia)	RLI	Rhodesian Light Infantry
ARBiH	Bosnia-Herzegovina Army	HSP	Croatian Party of Rights	RUF	Revolutionary United Front (Sierra Leone)
BSAP	British South Africa Police (Rhodesian)	HV	Croatian Army		
		HVO	Croatian Defence Council (in Bosnia-Herzegovina)	SADF	South African Defence Force
CCB	Civil Cooperation Bureau (S. African)			SAS	Special Air Service (British, & Rhodesian)
CF	Citizen Force (S. African reservists)	IFOR	Implementation Force (NATO, in former Yugoslavia. 1995)		
CPA	Coalition Provisional Authority (Iraq)			SDF	Syrian Democratic Forces
CRG	Control Risks Group	ISAF	International Security Assistance Force (in Afghanistan)	SFA	Security Force Auxiliaries (Rhodesian)
DRC	Democratic Republic of the Congo			SNAL	Suriname National Liberation Army
DST	Directorate Special Tasks (S. African)	IS	Islamic State	SWAPO	South West African People's Organization
ELNA	Angolan National Liberation Army	ISIS	Islamic State of Iraq/Syria (*Daesh*)	UÇK	Kosovo Liberation Army
ELP	Portuguese Liberation Army (Angola)	JNA	Yugoslav National Army	UN	United Nations
EO	Executive Outcomes	KMS	Keeni-Meeni Service**s**	UNITA	National Union for the Total Independence of Angola
FAA	Angolan Armed Forces	MPLA	Popular Movement for the Liberation of Angola		
FALA	Armed Forces for the Liberation of Angola			UNPROFOR	UN Protection Force (in former Yugoslavia, 1992)
		MPRI	Military Professional Resources Incorporated		
FAN	Armed Forces of the North (Chad)			USAID	United States Agency for International Development
FAPLA	People's Armed Forces for the Liberation of Angola	MUP	Croatian Interior Ministry		
		NATO	North Atlantic Treaty Organization	YPG	People's Defence Units (Kurdish)
FARC	Revolutionary Armed Forces of Colombia	NGO	non-governmental organization	ZANLA	Zimbabwe African National Liberation Army
		NIS	National Intelligence Service (S. African)	ZANU	Zimbabwe African National Union
FNLA	National Front for the Liberation of Angola	OAU	Organization of African Unity	ZAPU	Zimbabwe African People's Union
FRELIMO	Front for the Liberation of Mozambique	PATU	Police Anti-Terrorist Unit (Rhodesian)	ZIPRA	Zimbabwe People's Revolutionary Army
		PKK	Kurdistan Worker's Party		
GNA	Government of National Accord (Libya)	PLAN	People's Liberation Army of Namibia	ZNG	Croatian National Guard
		PMC	PMC/PMS private military/security company		

CONTENTS

SOLDIERS OF FORTUNE

MERCENARIES & MILITARY ADVENTURERS 1960–2020

A veteran of the war in disintegrating Yugoslavia in the 1990s, French former paratrooper 'Fran' (or 'Baba Sidar', as he was known to his young Kurdish comrades) later spent a total of 24 months with the Kurdish People's Defence Units (YPG) in northern Syria. He is seen here in October 2015, after an all-night vigil atop Djebel Abd al-Aziz. With the aid of American air support, his unit took part in reclaiming areas from ISIS/ Daesh control. The weapon is a 7.62mm Soviet AKM assault rifle, and the combat jacket is Syrian. See also Plates F2 & H3. (Private collection)

PREFACE: VENEZUELA, MAY 2020

Shortly before dawn on 3 May 2020, a mercenary-led operation was launched with the apparent aim of removing from power the increasingly autocratic President Nicolás Maduro of Venezuela, and replacing him with the more moderate opposition leader Juan Guaidó.

Installing Guaidó was clearly in the interests of Western powers, with companies eager to bid for lucrative contracts in Venezuela's energy and mining sectors during any rebuilding of the country's ruined economy. For those behind the coup, there was a further incentive: Maduro had been indicted in March by the US Department of Justice on charges of drug trafficking and narco-terrorism. Whoever could seize Maduro would be entitled to claim a $15 million reward posted by the US Drug Enforcement Agency, and other bounties were offered for the capture of his key associates.

A leading figure behind events was named as Jordan Goudreau, a Canadian-born American citizen, a decorated ex-'Green Beret' of the US Army Special Forces, and the founder of a Florida-based security risk management company, Silvercorp USA. Also involved were two other American ex-servicemen, Luke Denman and Airan Berry, both with links to Silvercorp. They were to lead an assault force comprising some 60 Venezuelan expatriates who, after training in neighbouring Colombia, were mobilized for the task.

From the outset, the attempt seems to have been grossly mismanaged. Venezuelan authorities were well aware of Goudreau's project, and in March 2020 Colombian police had seized a cache of weapons and tactical equipment intended for the coup. Associated Press had even released a detailed report about Goudreau and his accomplices on 1 May – two days before the operation commenced.

The outcome would have been comical but for the resulting deaths. When an initial pre-dawn beach landing from speedboats was attempted near the northern port city of La Guaira, Venezuelan security forces killed eight men and made two arrests. Denman and Berry were seized, along with half-a-dozen Venezuelans, apparently while attempting another landing – in daylight – by fishing boat. Within days, security forces had rounded up further suspects.

Denman and Berry were paraded on state television. They stated (no doubt under duress) that they were to have secured an airport to allow an aircraft to land, embark Maduro and fly him to the United States. It was not disclosed how they had intended to take the airport, or to overcome Maduro's considerable security force.

In 2020 the operation might have worked – as a Hollywood action movie. Toppling heads of state with a mercenary-led force is something that has succeeded in the past, when the world was considerably less sophisticated. Today, such ventures have little chance of success. So what future is there for the mercenary in the 21st century?

INTRODUCTION

Mercenaries – those willing to take employment abroad as soldiers, primarily for financial or other material gain – have existed since ancient times. The more recent phenomenon of this type of military adventurer is less easy to define. In the 20th century there were many who fought in foreign wars not for reward, but for a cause: consider the 'Internationals' of the Spanish Civil War (1936–39), and foreign volunteers in the ranks of both Allied and Axis forces during World War II.

In 1949 the term 'mercenary' was redefined under international law (see panel on p. 6), but the Geneva Conventions' description is clearly ambiguous. It does not mention, for example, those who fight abroad for reasons of ideology and/or religion. Neither has it been updated to take into account the private security section and its role in operations that were until recently the sole responsibility of national military forces.

In the first decades of the 21st century, in the United States, Britain and elsewhere, thousands of former military personnel have been recruited for high-risk ventures in Iraq and Afghanistan. Service providers became known as private military companies or PMCs. (Another oft-used but more disingenuous term is private security company, PSC.) Non-salaried personnel, who typically work for a day rate, are referred to as 'contractors'.

Is there any difference between a security contractor and a mercenary? Yes, according to the current definition – if, for example, an American citizen is contracted by an American company to partake in a war involving the United States. But what of those recruited by the same company from a nation that is not party to that conflict? What, then, constitutes a mercenary today?

This book considers the question, beginning with white volunteers who fought on behalf of black African leaders in the former Belgian Congo in the 1960s – probably the best-known mercenary force of the 20th century. It continues by looking at those who have served in the armed forces of countries other than their own (notably in Rhodesia, South

Peter McAleese, a Scotsman with a lifetime's military experience, is shown here while serving in the South African Defence Force as Company Sergeant Major of Pathfinder Company, 44 Parachute Brigade. He had joined the British Army in 1960 at the age of 17, serving alternating spells with 1st Bn, Parachute Regiment and D Sqn, 22 SAS during the 1960s, including tours in Aden and Borneo, before leaving the British Army as a staff sergeant in 1969. After a spell with 'Colonel Callan's' ill-fated mercenaries in Angola in 1976, he served with the Rhodesian SAS and the British South Africa Police Special Branch. (Dennis Croukamp)

Africa, and during the break-up of Yugoslavia) – men who served under the same terms and conditions and for the same meagre pay as every other soldier, and who therefore cannot be defined as mercenaries under Article (c) of the quoted Geneva Protocol. We also cover some more traditional 'old-school' mercenary operations, such as the abortive coup attempt in the Seychelles in 1981. We then examine the emergence and changing face of PMCs in Iraq and Afghanistan, and, finally, consider those who have fought against Islamist extremists in the Middle East.

AFRICA

THE CONGO
Katanga, 1960–63

On 30 June 1960 the Belgian Congo celebrated independence following 52 years of colonial rule. Within days there was turmoil, with President Joseph Kasa-Vubu and Prime Minister Patrice Lumumba unable to control the vast nation's many diverse tribes. An uprising within the ranks of the *Force Publique* (soon to be renamed the Congolese National Army – *l'Armée Nationale Congolaise*, ANC) led to Belgian military intervention, with mutineers disarmed and disbanded. However, in the mineral-rich south-eastern province of Katanga, troops loyal to the regional leader Moïse Tshombe were retained as his own army – *la Gendarmerie Katangaise*. On 11 July, as European residents were subjected to an increasing wave of violence throughout the Congo, Tshombe proclaimed the secession of Katanga.

These are some of the first mercenaries (or 'volunteers') to arrive in Katanga in 1961. They are uniformly kitted out with Belgian camouflage smocks copied from the British Denison pattern, and bush hats with a Katanga *Gendarmerie* badge (see Plate A1). The weapons are 7.62mm NATO FN rifles. (Nigel Osborn)

Two weeks after independence, the first troops of a United Nations peacekeeping force (ONUC) began to arrive, preparatory to taking over from departing Belgian forces. Soon afterwards, South Kasai was also declared an autonomous state by its provincial leader, Albert Kalonji. Disappointed by the ineffectiveness of the UN, Lumumba sought to resolve matters by turning to Russia for aid. Soon, his forces were sufficiently equipped to overrun Kasai, but an attempt to reclaim neighbouring Katanga failed.

Tshombe faced immediate threats not just from the Congolese central government in Léopoldville (Kinshasa) and the UN, but also from the Baluba, his tribal and political rivals in northern Katanga. His solution was to bolster his forces with white mercenaries – a move that was welcomed by Katanga's powerful Belgian-operated mining industry and resident European community.

On 14 September 1960, discord within the Léopoldville government led to the ANC chief of staff, Col Joseph Désiré Mobutu, taking control in a bloodless coup, and expelling Lumumba's Soviet and Communist-bloc advisers. Lumumba would be assassinated in captivity a few months later. In response, Lumumbists under Antoine Gizenga formed a rival government in Stanleyville (Kisangani) in the north-eastern Orientale Province.

This unidentified volunteer of Mike Hoare's 5 Commando in the Congo carries a 7.62mm NATO FN MAG belt-fed general-purpose machine gun; capable of firing at up to 1,000rpm, this has impressive stopping power. He wears 5 Cdo's green beret with the ANC brass badge, a Belgian smock in 'brush-stroke' camouflage, green drab trousers, and brown double-buckle boots. (James D. N. MacKenzie)

In February 1961, Kasa-Vubu was re-appointed as president, and in August the now-MajGen Mobutu replaced interim premier Joseph Iléo with Cyrille Adoula. Before long, the rival regimes in Léopoldville and Stanleyville were reconciled by means of a division of spoils, with key posts assigned to Gizenga and his political ally Christophe Gbenye. Unsurprisingly, such an arrangement did not sit easily with Moïse Tshombe.

By this time, 500 or more Belgian, French and English-speaking mercenaries were employed in Katanga, as well as Belgian officers seconded on contract to the *Gendarmerie*. At the end of August 1961 the UN conducted an operation to rid the *Gendarmerie* of foreign irregular and regular military personnel. Several hundred were expelled (although many would return and resume their activities). On 13 September, UN troops seized control of key points throughout Katanga. The next day, a combined mercenary/ Katangese force responded with the first in a series of assaults, against a UN company of Irish troops (A Coy, 35th Bn) at Jadotville. The attacking forces suffered heavy losses over several days, but the garrison was eventually forced to surrender (none had been killed, and the prisoners were exchanged a month later).

There followed a brief lull until 5 December 1961. Mercenaries captured by the UN were still being deported, but recruiting continued. This volatile situation continued for another year, before the UN demanded an end to Katanga's secession. When the ultimatum was rejected, UN troops went on the offensive. Tshombe's mercenaries and several thousand Katangese *gendarmes* were forced to withdraw across the southern border into the Portuguese colony of Angola. (The mercenaries included a French veteran of the Navy and colonial police who called himself Bob Denard, leading a small

1er Choc assault unit.) In mid-January 1963, Tshombe finally conceded defeat and went into exile; Katanga was reintegrated as a province of the Congo, and for a while enjoyed a period of relative calm.

The Congo, 1964–68

Early in 1964 there was an uprising in the Kwilu region of western Congo, instigated primarily by Pierre Mulele, who had received military training in China. Spearheaded by a force of teenage *jeunesse*, the revolt of the *Simba* ('Lions') rapidly spread. The UN, with no enthusiasm for continued involvement in the region, withdrew from the Congo on 30 June. At the same time, President Kasa-Vubu terminated Cyrille Adoula's premiership, prior to entrusting Moïse Tshombe – returned from voluntary exile in Spain – with forming a new Congolese government. Tshombe attempted to resolve the worsening crisis by negotiation; however, by August 1964 rebel leaders were in control of more than half the country, which they renamed the Popular Republic of the Congo *(la République populaire du Congo)*.

For Tshombe, the answer was to again employ a force of white mercenaries. He entrusted the task to Jeremiah ('Jerry') Puren, a World War II veteran of the South African Air Force and the RAF. Puren had been a mercenary platoon commander in Katanga, and later chief of the embryo Katangese Air Force. He was now to head air operations, and would also arrange initial recruitment of mercenaries. Puren reached out to another ex-Katanga mercenary, South African-resident former British Army officer Mike Hoare, who was given the rank of major and invited to create a mercenary unit to spearhead a ground offensive by Tshombe's *gendarmes*.

Although more than 1,000 men had been recruited, only 38 arrived at Kamina air base in time for Hoare's first operation. When told that they were to go straight into action, nine of them promptly resigned, but Hoare

The date and place are unidentified, but this photo shows a volunteer of 5 Cdo and a dead insurgent, the latter with what looks like a 7.62mm SKS rifle. While they might ambush road columns, enemy forces who stood to fight had little chance against Hoare's experienced, well-organized and better-equipped mercenaries. (James D. N. MacKenzie)

chose to press on. His plan was to fly his force to Kamipini, then move by road to Moba, before boating 100 miles (160km) north along Lake Tanganyika to Albertville (Kalimié). Once there, Hoare intended to secure the nearby airfield, await the landing of reinforcements, and then advance on the town.

In the event, Hoare departed Moba in late August with just 22 men (having combed out several whom he considered unsuitable). Furthermore, he deviated from the intended plan, which left him without reinforcements. Even so, two amphibious assaults were attempted; both failed, and two mercenaries lost their lives. By 1 September, Albertville was relieved by the ANC and hundreds of Belgian nationals were saved, but for Maj Hoare and his 5 Commando it was an ignominious beginning.

5 Commando, 1964–65

Hoare and his men retired to Kamina, where more than 500 volunteers had now assembled. Those who were accepted were organized into 40-man sub-units also termed 'commandos', and subjected to firm discipline during an intensive training programme. Responsibility for logistics and administration was taken over by seconded Belgian Army personnel. When they next deployed, the mercenaries would be much better prepared.

5 Commando would eventually comprise eight sub-units designated 51 to 58 Commandos, each 30 to 40 strong and (ideally) including two officers and three sergeants. Subordinate Commandos frequently operated independently of one another; they relied on speed, surprise and superior firepower, and used armed jeeps as the vanguard during assaults.

The first major success was achieved against numerically superior Simba at Lisala in the north by a company of ANC and 51 Cdo under 2nd Lt Gary Wilson. After he had been reinforced, Wilson continued east to Bumba, arriving shortly before the end of October and thus relieving the pressure on Gemena to the north-west.

Hoare's men would be deployed throughout the Congo, on one occasion operating in conjunction with intervening Belgian regular forces. On 24 November 1964, Belgian paratroopers descended on the outskirts of Stanleyville from USAF C-130E Hercules transports (Operation 'Red Dragon'). They secured the airport and pushed towards the town proper, though not before the Simba had massacred many inhabitants. 5 Commando arrived later in the day, by which time the battle was effectively over.

By January 1965, the mercenaries of 5 Commando were nearing the end of their six-month contracts. When Hoare was asked to raise a new 5 Cdo to secure the rest of Orientale Province he agreed, and was promoted to lieutenant-colonel. He would be assisted by two Britons from his original team, Maj Alastair Wicks and Capt John Peters. A new base was established at Bunia, west of Lake Albert, and on 15 March 1965 the 270-strong 5 Cdo commenced operations in the north-east.

After six months of successful operations, Hoare was offered a third contract, this time to overcome rebel resistance in the Fizi–Baraka region on the provincial border of south Kivu and north Katanga. Confronting him was a determined enemy, well-equipped and properly led. During a recent rebel raid on Bendera, between Fizi and Albertville, one of those killed had turned out to be a Cuban adviser.

One battalion, with its base at Albertville, was to be raised for service in the Fizi–Baraka area, and Maj Johnstone was promised his own battalion with which to safeguard the northern sector. In addition, the new 5 Cdo was to include a sub-unit of 30 men to crew an 80-foot gunboat (the *Ermans*), and six patrol torpedo (PT) boats to help police the lake border with Tanzania. Air support was available from about a dozen T-28 Trojans, four twinengine B-26 medium bombers (redesignated World War II A-26 Invaders), and a Bell helicopter.

In October 1965, President Kasa-Vubu dismissed Tshombe, appointing as prime minister-designate Évariste Kimba. With the tacit support of the CIA, LtGen Mobutu then ousted Kasa-Vubu in a bloodless coup on 24 November, and declared himself president, with Col Léonard Mulamba as the new premier. For Mike Hoare, it was time to depart the Congo, but his command passed to John Peters, and 5 Cdo, together with the French-speaking 6 Cdo now led by Maj Bob Denard, continued to serve Mobutu. (Denard had returned to the Congo in 1964 after a spell with the royalist forces in the Yemen.) Several mercenary officers, including the Belgian planter Jean 'Black Jack' Schramme, commanded other predominantly Katangese units of the ANC.

Mutinies, 1966–68

On 23 July 1966, an estimated 1,000 Katangese troops in Kisangani (formerly Stanleyville) revolted in support of the exiled Tshombe. With the exception of about 100 renegades from 6 Cdo, the majority of Denard's force, together with Peters' 5 Cdo, remained loyal to Mobutu. In September, Denard's men went on the offensive, attacking rebel Katangese and mercenaries alike and compelling them to withdraw from Kisangani, which effectively

April 1965, Basoko, Orientale Province: a rebel prisoner is questioned by an ANC captain (right), watched by a mercenary probably of 6 Commando. (Left) is a French officer, who commanded T-6 Texan (Harvard) aircraft based at Bumba. From 1962 until 1968 the Congolese Air Force was partly organized by the American CIA, which provided T-28 Trojan trainers armed for ground-attack work, originally with US civilian and later with anti-Communist Cuban exile aircrew and mechanics. (Bob Houcke)

ended the uprising. No doubt as a result of 6 Cdo's partial mutiny, Mobutu subsequently began to dismantle his mercenary force. John Peters resigned his command in March 1967, and Georg Schroeder, a South African former paratrooper, took over until 5 Cdo was disbanded about a month later. 6 Commando was reduced to about 500 men.

Mobutu had good reason to be concerned about the trustworthiness of his hired guns. Increasing concern over his ruthless purge of political opponents would lead to an attempted coup d'état, initiated by Schramme and also involving Bob Denard and Jerry Puren, with the intention of reinstating Tshombe. The operation, scheduled for the morning of 1 July 1967, was briefly delayed when, on 30 June, the exiled Tshombe was kidnapped, flown to Algeria, and imprisoned. Even so, it was thought that if a caretaker government was installed it could demand his release. The attempted take-over commenced at dawn on 5 July. Success was dependent on the seizure of Katanga Province, but the mercenaries were unable to overcome Mobutu's forces, despite the defection of some of the latter. Outnumbered and outmanoeuvred, they were besieged in Bukavu from August. Those who could do so withdrew in November into neighbouring Rwanda (about 120 who had been taken prisoner were released on 23 April 1968). Ex-President Tshombe died (or was murdered) in Algeria in June 1969.

Aftermath

Mobutu continued to rule his nation with customary ruthlessness. Political opponents, real or imaginary, were swiftly dealt with, and the economy was systematically looted. In 1971 the Congo was renamed Zaire, and the dictator Africanized his own name to Mobutu Sése Séko Kuku Ngbendu Wa Za Banga.

After having been in power for three decades, and no doubt recalling the achievements of Hoare's 5 Commando, in the late 1990s President Mobutu Sése Séko once more sought the assistance of white mercenaries. This time it was to safeguard his regime from an uprising by predominantly Zairean Banyamulenge Tutsi rebels led by Laurent-Désiré Kabila, an opponent of Mobutu since the former's pro-Lumumbist days in the early 1960s. Contemporary media reports suggest that by early 1997 the Zairean Army had been joined by up to 300 mercenaries; Group Alpha was made up of Frenchmen and Belgians, including veterans of Bob Denard's Comorian Presidential Guard (see below, 'The Comoros'), and Group Bravo of Krajina Serbs (see below, 'The Break-Up of Yugoslavia '). However, Kabila's Alliance of Democratic Forces for the Liberation of Congo (l'Alliance des forces démocratiques pour la libération du Congo – ADFL) proved unstoppable. On 17 May 1997, Kabila assumed control of Zaire, which was immediately renamed the Democratic Republic of the Congo ((la République démocratique du Congo – RDC).

In September 1997, four months after he was obliged to flee, Mobutu

4 July 1965, at Aketi west of Buta: a mortar team of LtCol Roger Lamouline's 6 Commando dissuade rebels from interfering during a helicopter medevac. The mostly-Belgian, French and Italian 6 Cdo had sub-units designated Groupes 60 –65 and Para, of which the latter was the most effective. In November 1965 command of 6 Cdo passed to Maj Bob Denard, who retained it until July 1967. Note the French 'Bigeard' caps and camouflage uniforms, with red shoulder-strap slides. 5 and 6 Cdos formed the spearhead of the ANC's largely Katangese 5th Mech Bde; its 7-10 Cdos were locally recruited, with seconded Belgian officers (who also formed the brigade staff) or mercenary leaders. The planter Jean Schramme raised and commanded 10 Commando. (Bob Houcke)

Sése Séko died in exile in the Moroccan capital, Rabat. President Laurent Kabila was himself assassinated in January 2001. He was succeeded by his son, Joseph, who ruled the troubled RDC until 2019.

RHODESIA
Initial clashes, 1964–66
In Rhodesia, a worsening crisis in the mid-1960s would develop into a decisive war between black and white Africans. The origins of the Rhodesian War were rooted in late-19th century colonialism and the legacy of African resentment. In the early 1960s two rival nationalist groups emerged: the Zimbabwe African People's Union (ZAPU) under Joshua Nkomo, strongest among the Ndbele people; and the Zimbabwe African National Union (ZANU) headed, initially, by the Rev Ndbaningi Sithole and later by Robert Mugabe, which was strongest among the Mashona. Both movements campaigned for black majority rule, but were hindered in their efforts by political differences and tribal rivalries.

ZAPU was outlawed by the Rhodesian government in September 1962, and replaced temporarily by the People's Caretaker Council (PCC). As a result of continuing internecine violence both the PCC and ZANU were banned two years later. Prominent nationalists, including Nkomo, Sithole and Mugabe, spent a decade in detention, during which time ZAPU and ZANU were directed by various lieutenants from new headquarters in neighbouring Zambia.

In July 1964 a unit of ZANU's military wing, the Zimbabwe African National Liberation Army (ZANLA), ambushed a white family in their car and murdered Petrus Oberholzer, in the first act of terrorism in Rhodesia since the 1890s. While it was an isolated case, the killing had a profound effect on the country's close-knit white community. Since the British Labour government of Harold Wilson was unsupportive, on 11 November 1965 Rhodesian Prime Minister Ian Smith severed ties with Britain by a Unilateral Declaration of Independence (UDI). Five months later, on 28 April 1966, security forces killed seven ZANLA insurgents in a skirmish that would mark, for ZANU, the beginning of *Chimurenga* – their war of liberation.

Intensification, and the first 'externals', 1972–74
Relatively low-key conflict continued for six years, until 21 December 1972, when ZANLA struck first at Altena Farm in north-east Rhodesia, and then at an adjoining farm to which Altena's de Borchgrave family had been evacuated. When troops responded soon afterwards, a corporal in the Rhodesian Light Infantry was fatally injured when a vehicle detonated a ZANLA landmine, and a trooper lost both legs.

Events deteriorated when the Front for the Liberation of Mozambique (*Frente de Libertação de Moçambique* – FRELIMO), which had been battling

September 1965, at Baraka on the west bank of Lake Tanganyka: LtCol Mike Hoare (centre) with the wounded Capt John Peters (right), shortly before Peters took over command of 5 Cdo after Hoare completed his third contract. Born in India of Irish stock, Hoare had joined the London Irish Rifles early in World War II; later commissioned, he transferred to 2nd Reconnaissance Regt in 1941, and saw action in 1944–45 at Kohima (where 2nd Recce fought mainly as infantry) and in Burma, ending the war with the rank of major.
On his upper sleeve Hoare displays a 'Wild Geese' patch: red '5 COMMANDO' in an arc, above a blue goose flying left to right, on pale khaki backing. Officers and warrant officers wore green shoulder-strap slides, with a commando dagger above Belgian-style ranking. (Bob Houcke)

against Portuguese colonial rule since 1962, consolidated its gains in the central Tete Province, from where ZANLA was now able to operate in force. Clearly, for the Rhodesian security forces, the solution was to hit the enemy in his base camps and staging areas before he could infiltrate Rhodesia. Cross-border undercover operations by the Rhodesian C Sqn, Special Air Service had, in fact, commenced as early as the mid-1960s. Security forces were also already engaged in 'hot pursuits' into Mozambique, and events led the Rhodesian government to authorize an increasing number of 'externals', as cross-border operations were termed.

Less than three weeks after the attack at Altena, ZANLA murdered two civilians at Hartley, and abducted another who was force-marched into Mozambique before being held prisoner in Tanzania. This was the pretext for the first officially sanctioned parachute insertion of SAS troops into Mozambique. The operation commenced on 19 January 1973 and continued, with the approval of Mozambique's Portuguese administration, for nearly a month.

It would be seven more years before Rhodesia's war was finally over. The landlocked country had a relatively small army and air force. The Army comprised five combat formations. Operating throughout the country, the three-battalion Rhodesian African Rifles (RAR) was manned by black Africans led by white officers, until the integration of black officers late in the war. 1st Battalion, Rhodesian Light Infantry (RLI) would evolve as an airborne fast-reaction unit. C Squadron (Rhodesian) Special Air Service – retitled in 1978 as 1 Special Air Service Regt (Rhodesia) – was a select unit involved primarily in external operations. The SAS and RLI were the only units not to be racially integrated. The Selous Scouts specialized in intelligence-gathering, tracking and infiltrating guerrilla units, and manning covert observation posts; many of its operators were turned 'terrs'. The Army also included Grey's Scouts (horse-mounted infantry), an armoured car regiment, artillery, engineers and essential support units.

B

RHODESIA, 1966–79

(1): Trooper Barry Gribbin, Rhodesian Light Infantry
This American volunteer from Miami, Florida served in Support Cdo, 1st Bn, RLI. In the bush, RLI 'troopies' tended to wear whatever they found practical, such as this T-shirt and Army-issue trousers in the distinctive Rhodesian camouflage pattern, and American tropical boots. The drab-green and maroon fibre dog-tags were similar to those worn by British service personnel. Gribbin is seen here with a captured 7.62mm RPK light support weapon. For self-defence he also carries a privately-purchased 9mm Smith & Wesson Model 39 pistol and spare magazines, in a Galco 'Jackass' shoulder rig configured for left-handed shooters: 'Great pistol… saved my bacon during a split-casing stoppage with my FN.'

(2) Sergeant Wally Insch, Selous Scouts
This Rhodesian senior NCO is kitted out in a style typical of the RLI, to enable him to be inserted with them during a routine Fireforce operation. He has acquired a Rhodesian Air Force 'jump suit', a popular item for those who could get one. An issue face veil is secured around his head. It was common to supplement or replace inferior issue webbing with enemy items. Captured chest webbing designed for Kalashnikov magazines could be modified to better accommodate shorter FN rifle magazines. In this case, the 'Chicom'-type chest webbing has two additional pouches attached below the front. The boots are canvas with rubber toecaps and smooth anti-tracking soles. The handset of either an A63 or A76 radio is clipped to the right shoulder brace of the webbing, the radio itself being carried in a small backpack. He is armed with the standard-issue 7.62mm FN rifle, with the butt attached to his webbing with para-cord and a snap hook.

(3) Paul French, Rhodesian Special Air Service
This Englishman was in 21 SAS prior to going to Rhodesia and passing selection for both the Rhodesian SAS and, later, the Selous Scouts. He is depicted here in early 1976, during a camp attack 'external' in Mozambique. Shirt and trousers are standard issue, worn with Bata Super Takkie anti-tracking boots. Apart from the Chinese Type 56 (SKS) chest rig, web equipment is British ex-21 SAS, consisting of a quick-release heavy drop belt, modified 58 Pattern yoke, and (shortened) Bren magazine pouches. The rifle is camouflage-painted, and its sling is braided para-cord: 'Real slings with buckles made too much noise.' A small pack (not illustrated) would also have been carried. After the Rhodesian War, French went on to serve in South Africa in 6 Reconnaissance Commando, and later worked as a security contractor in Iraq.

Rhodesia, probably mid-1976: South African-born Earl 'Jake' Harper-Ronald, photographed just after a lengthy external deployment – he served with both the Rhodesian SAS and the Selous Scouts. Emigrating to Rhodesia at an early age, Jake did his national service in the Royal Rhodesia Regt, before travelling to the UK and joining the Parachute Regt, returning to Rhodesia in 1974. After the war he joined the BSAP, before working for various intelligence agencies, including the British, and subsequently as a security contractor in Iraq.
In Rhodesia, FN rifles were camouflage–painted, usually in two shades of green; note also the non-regulation sling made from para-cord. The 58 Pattern webbing is also non-issue, recalling Jake's previous British service. (Private collection)

The racially-integrated British South Africa Police (BSAP – the anachronistic title was retained), besides being responsible for law and order, included Police Support Units (PSU), and the Police Anti-Terrorist Unit (PATU, or 'Blackboots'). The war also spawned unorthodox formations such *Pfumo re Vanhu* ('Spear of the People'), better known as Security Force Auxiliaries (SFA) – a militia whose primary loyalty lay with moderate black nationalist leaders.

The Air Force consisted of seven squadrons, and had two main operating bases at New Sarum (Salisbury) and Thornhill (Gwelo) plus a number of Forward Air Fields (FAFs). Eventually, it would have a modest number of jet combat aircraft: Hawker Siddeley Hunters, De Havilland Vampires and English Electric Canberras. Other fixed-wing machines included the Douglas DC-3 Dakota, and the Cessna-Reims FTB-337G 'Lynx'. The Aérospatiale Alouette III was the only available helicopter before 1978, which saw the arrival, probably from Israel, of several Agusta-Bell AB-205A 'Cheetahs'.

Foreign volunteers

The Rhodesian security forces attracted a considerable number of volunteers from all over the world. Most, if not all, believed they were fighting for a just cause against a ruthless Communist-inspired enemy. But Rhodesia also presented an opportunity to participate in a real shooting war, something that many professional soldiers had long been denied in the service of their own countries. Army recruits signed on for an initial three-year term, and whatever their background virtually all applicants had to undergo selection and/or training. The great majority were from the English-speaking countries, serving under exactly the same regulations and for the same pay as Rhodesians.

Opposing forces and operations, 1974–79

In April 1974 a left-wing coup d'état in Portugal heralded the end of colonial rule in Angola and Mozambique the following year. In the latter, FRELIMO soon formed a transitional government, before officially taking control of the country in June 1975. These developments were as beneficial for ZANLA as they were disastrous for Rhodesia, now faced with the impossible task of defending 680 miles (1,100km) of the eastern border with Mozambique.

By 1977 the war had spread throughout Rhodesia. ZANLA, continuing to operate out of Mozambique, remained dominant among the Mashona people in the eastern and central areas of Rhodesia, where ZANU drew much of its support. The use of bases in Zambia to the north-west and Botswana to the south-west enabled the largely Ndebele ZAPU's Zimbabwe People's Revolutionary Army (ZIPRA) to remain active in the north and west.

In the bush, nationalist guerrillas were lightly equipped with modern weapons including AK and SKS rifles, light machine guns (typically the RPK and RPD), RPG-2 and RPG-7 shoulder-fired rocket launchers, and Soviet F1 and Chinese stick grenades. Most insurgents wore civilian clothing, and would often mingle with local tribespeople in an effort to evade security forces. While many lacked basic military skills, some had undergone training in Communist-bloc and other sympathetic countries. ZANLA was supported primarily by China and ZIPRA by the Soviet Union; this was reflected in their weapons and equipment. An impressive arsenal of heavy weapons defended guerrilla base camps, and during external operations the security forces might have to contend with mortars and 12.7mm and 14.5mm heavy machine guns. Towards the end of the war heavier weapons, including the 122mm multiple rocket launcher system, were used against Rhodesian raids.

As the war intensified, the Rhodesian military perfected a tactic known as 'Fireforce', a major advantage of which was its flexibility. Based at a FAF or a temporary base, Fireforce reacted swiftly to terrorist incidents or sightings, and became a speciality of the RLI and RAR. A typical operation might comprise a DC-3 'Para-Dak' (typically with 16 paratroopers), three Alouette III 'G-cars' (each able to transport a four-man 'stick'), and one 'K-car'. An Air Force gunner/technician sat on the port side of each G-car manning single or twin Browning machine guns. The K-car was the command and gunship, equipped with multiple machine guns or a 20mm cannon; besides allowing the unit commander to control events from above, it could also provide fire support. Further back-up might be provided by at least one Lynx, armed with Browning MGs and rockets, and with the capability of dropping 'frantan' (napalm) bombs. Fixed wing aircraft sometimes provided additional ground-attack support.

The Selous Scouts and SAS conducted numerous 'externals', often operating in small teams. During the mid to late 1970s more ambitious large-scale raids were undertaken by both units, as well as by the RLI. Troops carried whatever was necessary to sustain them during operations. Paul French described the contents of his rucksack during an external in Zambia in October 1979: 'On the Chambeshi Bridges job it carried 10 days' rations, 5 days' water, sleeping bag, bivvie bag, Big Means (TR 48 HF set), Small Means (A76 VHF set), spare battery packs, cooker, one mess tin, set of civvie kit, Claymore mine, spare ammunition and grenades.'

The professionalism of the Rhodesian security forces is reflected in their fatality rate, which remained fairly low throughout the war. In contrast,

Rhodesia, late 1970s: members of Support Cdo, 1 RLI carry out equipment checks before boarding a 3 Sqn DC-3 'Paradak' at Grand Reefs forward airfield following a Fireforce call-out. In Rhodesia, paratroopers always jumped with weapons secured by their parachute harness on the right side. One of the MAG gunners (left) is a British former trapeze artist; the other (far right, back to camera) is a native Canadian; and the Air Force despatcher wearing a T-shirt and shorts is from Australia. (Private collection)

17 April 1979, during a Fireforce call-out near Inyazura in eastern Rhodesia. This image first appeared, with a misleading caption, in a book published in 1981; it has also appeared on the internet, invariably as 'evidence of Rhodesian brutality'. In fact, as RLI troops were searching a kraal, an unsupervised and frightened toddler ran among them. Concerned for his safety, Australian Cpl Pete Binion, a Vietnam veteran and Support Cdo medic, picked up the child to get him out of harm's way, and handed him to the woman seen at the right. (Private collection)

a disproportionate number of insurgents were killed, wounded or captured, particularly during major Rhodesian cross-border strikes. Camps in Zambia and Mozambique were routinely targeted. Some externals were day-long affairs, during which a small force would be inserted by helicopter with specific tasks, before being airlifted back to Rhodesia. Other operations involved longer-term planning and preparation before deploying a strike force deep inside enemy territory for several days, with heavy air support.

Typical was Operation 'Dingo' launched in November 1977, which targeted the two most important ZANLA bases: to the east, Chimoio was some 40 miles (60km) inside Mozambique, while Tembué, to the north, was more than double that distance. Up to 9,000 ZANLA are believed to have been at Chimoio, with another 4,000 at Tembué. The assault force numbered less than 200 SAS and RLI, although with additional troops in reserve at rear-area locations. Air support was substantial and included transport and strike aircraft, as well as an impressive helicopter force. Chimoio was attacked first, then Tembué, and it was three days before the Rhodesians withdrew. One pilot and his aircraft were lost; one SAS trooper was killed, and several men were wounded. There are no reliable figures for insurgent casualties, but it is thought that literally thousands were killed and wounded.

In 1979 fighting intensified as the war entered its final phase, seeing an increasing number of cross-border operations. At the same time, the future of what had already been renamed Zimbabwe Rhodesia was being decided at the Lancaster House talks in London. On 21 December 1979 a ceasefire was announced, heralding the rise to power of Robert Mugabe and the beginning of the end for yet another decolonized African nation. The following year the new Zimbabwe government disbanded some of Rhodesia's finest units, including the Special Air Service, the Selous Scouts and the Rhodesian Light Infantry.

BIAFRA, 1968–70

In November 1967, even as the last Congo mercenaries withdrew across the Ruzizi river into Rwanda, another African war was underway. The previous May the province of Biafra had seceded from the Federation of Nigeria, and the secessionist leader Col Ojukwu would also hire mercenaries. Among them were Rolf Steiner from Germany and Armand Ianarelli from Corsica, both via the French Foreign Legion; South African-based Hugh 'Taffy' Williams, and 'Johnny' Erasmus from Rhodesia; Alexander Gay from Glasgow, via Schramme's 'Leopard Battalion' in the Congo; and even the ageing Count Carl Gustav von Rosen from Sweden, who emerged as something of a national hero after a brief spell leading fellow Swedes flying rocket-firing MFI-9B 'Minicons' in support of ground operations.

Under Steiner, a 4th Commando Brigade (later 'Division') was formed for the Biafran Army in 1968, but this differed fundamentally from the

Congo 5 and 6 Commandos: the rank-and-file were all local recruits, with the mercenaries serving purely in training and leadership roles. The three-battalion brigade initially numbered perhaps 3,000, and reportedly enjoyed high morale – until it suffered disproportionately high casualties, due largely to Biafra's chronic shortage of weapons and ammunition. Steiner's drunken insubordination led to his expulsion from Biafra in November 1968, after which only a handful of white instructors remained. (See MAA 507, *Modern African Wars (5): The Nigerian-Biafran War 1967–70.*)

ANGOLA, 1975–76

Background

During the mid-1970s three nationalist groups emerged in the rapidly crumbling Portuguese colony of Angola: Dr Agostinho Neto's Popular Movement for the Liberation of Angola (*Movimento Popular de Libertação de Angola* – MPLA); Jonas Savimbi's National Union for the Total Independence of Angola (*União Nacional para a Independência Total de Angola* – UNITA); and Holden Roberto's National Front for the Liberation of Angola (*Frente Nacional de Libertação de Angola* – FNLA). All had been united in an uneasy alliance against the common foe, but they were divided by tribal loyalties and political doctrines.

By June 1975, six months before the final withdrawal of Portuguese forces, MPLA – Soviet-backed, and assisted by Cuban advisers – was engaged in heavy fighting against both the other movements. UNITA was armed and equipped primarily by China, though it would later receive support from the United States and South Africa. FNLA had a useful ally in Zaire (President Mobutu Sése Séko was Holden Roberto's brother-in-law), and was also viewed with some favour by the United States. The prize for the victors would be control of a land rich in natural resources.

In August 1975, units of the South African Defence Force (SADF) infiltrated Angola in support of an FNLA-UNITA alliance, and to safeguard national interests in that country's Calueque/Ruacana hydroelectric complex. Operation 'Savannah' followed in October (see below, 'South Africa's Border War, 1966-89'), with SADF units invading southern Angola.

The South African intervention provoked Cuba to send tens of thousands of troops with heavy equipment to Angola. (It also resulted in declining support for FNLA and UNITA from hitherto sympathetic African nations.) Amid this turmoil, Angola celebrated its independence on 11 November 1975. Subsequently, MPLA announced the formation of a government under President Neto; FNLA and the then-weaker UNITA responded by forming a rival administration in their territory, under Holden Roberto.

The RLI, together with the Rhodesian African Rifles (RAR), also conducted 'externals' in Zambia and Mozambique. In April 1979, RLI Support Cdo undertook a day-long raid against a guerrilla camp near Malvernia, Chicuacuala District, in south-western Mozambique. By late afternoon most of the attack force had been airlifted back to Rhodesia. Those seen here were uncertain whether there was enough daylight remaining for them to be flown out, or if they would have to remain in Mozambique overnight. In the event, the crew of an Agusta-Bell 205A helicopter succeeded in evacuating them before nightfall. The trooper with a captured SKS rifle is Australian; two Rhodesians wear enemy field caps. (Private collection)

Monitoring events in far-off England were four ex-soldiers of the Parachute Regt: Nick Hall, Mick Wainhouse, and Greek-Cypriots Charlie Christodoulou and Costas Georgiou. In December 1975, Georgiou arrived in the Zairean capital, Kinshasa, with Donald Belford and Colin Taylor (representatives of FNLA in Britain). 'Doc' Belford, having had some medical training, was soon attending the sick and wounded in Angola, accompanied by Georgiou, who had by now adopted the *nom de guerre* 'Tony Callan'. The former paratrooper was now confronted by the extraordinary complexity of Angola's war. He encountered white Portuguese serving in FNLA's Angolan National Liberation Army (*Exército de Libertação Nacional de Angola* – ELNA), engaged in fighting MPLA's People's Armed Forces for the Liberation of Angola (*Forças Armadas Populares de Libertação de Angola* – FAPLA) – which itself had attracted some other Portuguese. Yet others had joined UNITA's Armed Forces for the Liberation of Angola (*Forças Armadas de Liberação de Angola* – FALA), while a final faction belonged to the Portuguese Liberation Army (*Exército de Libertação Português* – ELP), which had been formed by settlers dedicated to returning Angola to white rule.

Towards Christmas 1975, Belford and Taylor returned to England, while Callan remained at Carmona. When that town was taken by FAPLA and Cuban forces a few days later, Callan escaped to Negage, where he organized a fighting patrol to safeguard the town, and allegedly engaged enemy forces on a number of occasions.

'Colonel Callan'

In New Year 1976, Callan was joined by his friends Hall, Wainhouse and Christodoulou after they had returned to Kinshasa with Taylor. The latter seems to have departed again not long afterwards, leaving Callan and his colleagues with President Holden Roberto, who accompanied them across the border into

C

SOUTH AFRICAN DEFENCE FORCE, 1981–82
(1) Steve Biddlecombe, 32 Battalion
This volunteer, one of a number of ex-RLI who joined 32 Bn, is armed with a 7.62mm RPK (essentially a heavy-barrelled version of the AK-47 assault rifle), with a custom-made leather sling. Weapon, uniform and equipment are fairly typical for this unit's cross-border operations. (During larger 'externals' such as Op 'Protea', regulation 'nutria'-brown uniforms were usually worn and standard-issue weapons carried.) The bush shirt and trousers show a camouflage pattern that was unique to 32 Bn; based on the Portuguese M1960 2-c (itself copied from the old French M1947/56), it resembled that used by FAPLA forces in Angola. It was made in dry season (shown here) and wet season variants. Boots and bush hat are Rhodesian Army issue. Web equipment was worn according to personal preference – here, a captured 'ChiCom' chest rig suitable for 30-round magazines, plus an ammunition pouch attached to the web belt. At least one canteen would have been carried, with any remaining kit in a backpack left at a nearby temporary base (TB). Black and brown camouflage cream was often worn on exposed skin, helping white operators appear less distinguishable from SWAPO or FAPLA, at least from a distance.

(2) Mario Vidal, Reconnaissance Commandos
This Spanish volunteer had served in both the Spanish Legion (the 'Tercio') and French Foreign Legion before joining the Rhodesian Light Infantry, and was subsequently accepted into South Africa's special forces. Photographed while practising with an RPG-7, he wears SADF coveralls in 'nutria' brown with the top half undone and folded down, secured by its sleeves around the waist. The faded T-shirt is Rhodesian, while his cap, shoulder rig and lightweight boots are of unknown origins.

(3) Ken Gaudet, Pathfinder Company, 44 Parachute Brigade
Gaudet had joined the US Army at the age of 18. After Airborne training and an NCO Officer Candidate Course, he was shipped to Vietnam, where he served as a sergeant in 'Hawk' pacification teams (each team comprising about half-a-dozen American and Vietnamese ARVN troops). In 1979 he joined the Rhodesian Light Infantry, serving in Recce Troop of Support Commando. Subsequently he joined the exodus south, where he passed selection for Pathfinder Company, 44 Parachute Brigade. Uniform and equipment include 'nutria'-brown short-brimmed bush hat, coveralls and nylon chest webbing (all SADF issue), but supplemented with a US Army web belt and pouches. The wrist compass is Rhodesian Army issue. Footwear is non-regulation: Adidas trainers were more comfortable than boots, and left a sole pattern that was distinctly unmilitary. The weapon is the 5.56mm R4 assault rifle, a South African development of the Israeli Galil.

Mozambique, September 1979: seen at the end of the cross-border Operation 'Uric', French volunteer Henri Lepetit served in 1 RLI before passing SAS selection. Generally, Rhodesian security forces did not wear steel helmets, which were of limited use in bush warfare, and unpopular; this type is thought to have come from the SADF, and seems to resemble the French M1956 airborne pattern. Lepetit's weapon is a customized 7.62mm belt-fed RPD, with an ammunition-carrier secured with para-cord: 'versatile and dependable, [and it] stood me fast for the duration of the war.' (Private collection)

Angola. The ex-Paras evidently made an impression on the FNLA president. At São Salvador, he named Callan as his field commander for all military operations in the northern sector. Roberto then returned to Kinshasa, taking Nick Hall with him as his personal bodyguard. During the trip the president discussed with Hall the possibility of hiring more British mercenaries for his army, and presented him with cash to enable him to recruit 25 men.

Among those who signed up for the Angola venture was Dave Tomkins, a former burglar and safe-blower with no previous military experience. Notwithstanding this unpromising background, Tomkins would subsequently emerge as a well-respected figure. The 25 men also included Glaswegian Peter McAleese, formerly of the Parachute Regt and 22 SAS. McAleese and Tomkins were to become firm friends, developing a working relationship that would see them operating together in Colombia a decade later.

A number of would-be mercenaries withdrew before even reaching Africa. Those who arrived in Kinshasa were issued with boots, camouflage uniforms, web equipment and weapons – a mixture of 7.62mm FN rifles and .30cal M1/M2 carbines. The men were driven across the border into Angola, arriving at São Salvador. A pecking order was soon established under the commander, 'Colonel Callan'. Hall, Wainhouse and Christodoulou also became officers, as did McAleese; another ex-Para, 'Sammy' Copeland, was designated regimental sergeant major (RSM).

The mercenaries learned that they were to operate as four-man 'killer' teams for hunt-and-destroy missions against Cuban patrols. Thirteen Land Rovers were available, together with a Panhard M3/VTT armoured personnel carrier, a Dodge personnel carrier, a Panhard AML-90 armoured car, a Ferret scout car, a 3-ton Mercedes truck, and a heavy recovery vehicle. Only some of these vehicles were in good running order, and Chris Dempster, formerly of the Royal Artillery, was tasked with servicing those that were defective.

Summary executions

Georgiou/ 'Callan' was probably hoping to emulate the exploits of the Congo mercenaries of the 1960s. In the event, he and his men were to have no effect on the outcome of the war in Angola, with any minor achievements being overshadowed by one infamous event. In the Congo, there had been isolated incidents in which individual mercenaries had murdered others, but on nothing like the scale of what would take place in Angola.

At the end of January 1976, 96 recruits arrived in Kinshasa. Many had little or no military experience, and were noticeably less motivated than the original contingent. During their first parade some voiced misgivings; 23 opted out or were rejected by Callan as unsuitable. Under the supervision of two newly-appointed NCOs, they were relegated to fatigue duties at Maquela. During their first night there, an approaching vehicle with Chris Dempster and three other mercenaries aboard was misidentified by the panicky 'non-combatants'. They opened fire, albeit without causing

As well as infiltrating guerrilla bands and manning covert observation posts, Rhodesia's Selous Scouts also undertook cross-border operations, and this 2.5-ton Mercedes Unimog was photographed during one such 'external'. Crammed full of equipment and supplies, the vehicle also mounts a .50cal Browning M2 heavy machine gun at the front, and a .30cal Browning M1 at the near side. The bearded warriors typify the unit's image; note that one has apparently picked up an East German steel helmet along the way. (Dennis Croukamp)

casualties. All 25 of them then commandeered vehicles and headed for the Zairean border. They were stopped at Cuimba, where Terry Wilson (ex-Rhodesian SAS) had been put in charge of an FNLA detachment. The vehicles were re-routed, soon arriving at Callan's location on the São Salvador road where, having been advised by radio that Maquela had 'fallen', he had ordered his men to prepare defensive positions.

It was not long before the situation was clarified. On hearing how Dempster and his three colleagues had been mistakenly ambushed, Callan demanded to know who had fired first. When one man stepped forward, Callan shot him dead on the spot. At this, some of the other reluctant mercenaries changed their minds and offered to continue soldiering; others, less fortunate, were ordered to undress and climb on to a truck. In a valley a short distance away they were gathered in front of half-a-dozen mercenaries under RSM Copeland. Copeland opened fire, followed by the rest of the execution squad. When it was over, at least 11 men were dead.

Not long afterwards, Callan was wounded and taken prisoner. He was succeeded as FNLA field commander by Peter McAleese, who ordered an investigation into the killing of the non-combatants. As a result of its findings, Copeland was sentenced to death and shot.

Even as the situation deteriorated, mercenary reinforcements continued to arrive, including half-a-dozen from the United States, but by mid-February it was all but over. Surviving mercenaries fled for the safety of neighbouring Zaire. In June 1976, 13 captive mercenaries were subjected to a much-publicized show trial in Angola. Costas Georgiou, together

Angola, 1975–76: when 'Callan's' British mercenaries arrived and took service with Holden Roberto's FNLA movement, the situation on the ground was extremely complex. These are local Portuguese volunteer fighters wearing the insignia of FNLA's Angolan National Liberation Army (ELNA), one of a number of organizations battling Agostinho Neto's rival People's Armed Forces for the Liberation of Angola (FAPLA). (Don Carl Steffen/Gamma-Rapho via Getty Images)

South Africa's Border War, *c.* 1980: a member of 32 Battalion during a foot patrol in SW Africa or Angola. Compare with Plate C1; his kit is a mix of issue and non-regulation items, the cap indicating his former service in Rhodesia. The weapon is an RPK with a 75-round drum magazine. (Private collection)

with fellow Britons Derek Barker and Andrew McKenzie and an American, Daniel Gearhart, were condemned to death, and executed by firing squad on 10 July 1976. Two Americans and seven more Britons received prison sentences ranging from 16 to 30 years. Both Americans were released in December 1982, and the others in March 1984.

According to a list prepared by Peter McAleese, of 143 predominantly British mercenaries who arrived in Angola, some 29 were killed, wounded or reported missing.

Aftermath

In February 1976 the Organization of African Unity (OAU) recognized the MPLA's Republic of Angola, and the SADF's Operation 'Savannah' (see below) came to an end the following month. This did not end the fighting between MPLA and UNITA, which continued almost without pause for 27 years. (South Africa's preference for UNITA had hastened the end of Holden Roberto's FNLA as a major contender in the civil war.)

Between August 1993 and January 1996, mercenaries of the South African company Executive Outcomes assisted government forces in their efforts to defeat UNITA (see, 'Private Military Companies'). Following a ceasefire in November 1994, fighting resumed in mid-1997. Another ceasefire was negotiated after 67-year-old Jonas Savimbi was killed in action on 22 February 2002. The death of UNITA's leader further strengthened the hold of President José Eduardo dos Santos of MPLA, and brought some temporary respite to a troubled land.

SOUTH AFRICA'S BORDER WAR, 1966–89

Background

The Border War lasted from 1966 to 1989, and was fought in two adjoining territories: in northern Namibia, and southern Angola. In an open, largely arid wilderness, the two territories (and the local peoples, particularly the Ovambo) were divided by an essentially artificial east-west border line on the political map.

Under a League of Nations mandate, the former German South West Africa (SWA, now Namibia) had been administered by South Africa since December 1920. Four decades later, Britain's Conservative Prime Minister Harold Macmillan made it clear, in his 'Winds of Change' speech to the South African parliament on 3 February 1960, that his party was no longer supportive of white minority rule in African states.

Soon, the nationalist Ovambo People's Congress, founded in the 1950s, became the South West African People's Organization (SWAPO). By 1962 it had established headquarters in Lusaka, Zambia, and founded the People's Army for the Liberation of Namibia (PLAN). Recruits were given basic training in Tanzania, with many undergoing advanced and/or specialist courses in countries such as Algeria, Egypt, Cuba, the USSR, North Korea and China. At the same time, SWAPO forged links with the anti-Portuguese UNITA movement in southern Angola.

In 1965 half-a-dozen PLAN insurgents entered Ovamboland (SWA), where they started a programme of political indoctrination and provided elementary military instruction for potential recruits. An initially low-intensity conflict was initiated by another group in mid-1966. Initial security operations were adequately handled by the South African Police, together with air support. In spring 1974, the SADF took over border protection (alongside continuing Police operations, including, from 1979, by racially-integrated SWAPOL-TIN Koevoet units). Inevitably, hostilities escalated.

The end of the Rhodesian War in December 1979 precipitated a migration south by a good number of seasoned bush-fighters. Initially, at least, the South Africans were happy to employ such men. For some Rhodesians, facing an uncertain future in a land ruled by their erstwhile enemy, the SADF offered a welcome transition. For others it was an opportunity to continue to do battle, albeit for another government and against a different foe. Many former members of Rhodesia's land forces opted for one of three élite SADF units: the Reconnaissance Commandos, 32 Battalion, and Pathfinder Company of 44 Parachute Brigade.

Recces units

In October 1972 an innovative South African officer, Maj Jan Breytenbach, had founded 1 Reconnaissance Commando. By the mid-1970s three more Commandos were operational: 2 Recce was a Citizen Force (CF) unit; 4 Recce specialized in amphibious operations; and 5 Recce was a predominantly black African unit. In February/March 1980, about 100 ex-Rhodesian SAS formed 6 Recce, and in April, 3 Recce was activated with some 120 ex-Selous Scouts. Rhodesian special forces operators were exempt from 'selection', an arduous process designed to prepare the right kind of soldiers for covert operations in enemy territory, but they were required to undergo a parachute conversion course. In January 1981 the Reconnaissance Commandos were reorganized, and absorbed as sub-units into Reconnaissance Regiments.

Like the former Rhodesian SAS and Selous Scouts, the Recce Cdos/ Regts had their own distinctive roles. Tasks typically involved working deep inside enemy territory. Teams varied in size, and might be deployed as part of

South African Col Jan Breytenbach (left) first served in the South African Army in the 1950s, before travelling to Britain and joining the Royal Navy, qualifying as a Fleet Air Arm navigator and seeing active service at Suez in 1956. In 1961 he re-enlisted in the SADF, and would later be instrumental in creating the Recce Commandos, 32 Bn, and Pathfinder Company. Here, the crew of his Pathfinder Company modified Toyota Land Cruiser are Americans Dave Barr (centre), the gunner, and driver Lang Price. Barr had been a US Marines helicopter door-gunner in Vietnam, and went on to serve in both the Israeli Defence Force and the Rhodesian Army; Lang Price had served in the RLI. In August 1981 their command vehicle ran over a landmine; Breytenbach and Price were able to walk away, but Barr lost both legs, and the English signaller Graham Gillmore (ex-Grenadier Guards) was also seriously injured. (Dennis Croukamp)

Members of SADF 12 Cdo (formerly 6 Recce) during urban live-fire training preparatory to Operation 'Beanbag' in January 1981. (Left to right:) L/Cpl Jim Park, who was killed during the raid; Sgt Rob Riddell, ex-Rhodesian SAS, and Cpl 'Jon' Caffin. The latter, formerly of the French Air Force and the RLI, had passed SAS selection in Rhodesia early in 1980, which also made him eligible for service in South African special forces. Their equipment includes German Bundeswehr paratrooper helmets, South African 'nutria' coveralls, various styles of chest and belt webbing, and AK rifles. (Private collection)

a combined-forces cross-border operation or during a specific unit mission. An example of the latter was Operation 'Beanbag', which was carried out by former Rhodesian personnel in January 1981, with the primary objective of seizing members of the African National Congress (ANC) based in Mozambique. Following weeks of rehearsals, and after having already aborted one attempt, members of what had been 6 Recce (by this time 12 Cdo, part of 1 Recce Regt) entered Mozambique in a convoy disguised as FRELIMO, and drove overnight to Matola, a residential suburb of Maputo. There, several houses were targeted; a number of ANC were killed and three were taken prisoner. Three commandos lost their lives: Sgt Ian Suttil from the UK (former Royal Marines and Rhodesian SAS), and Rhodesians Sgt Robert Hutchison (ex-RLI) and L/Cpl Jim Park (ex-Rhodesian SAS). Another operator was severely wounded.

In post-apartheid South Africa, 4 and 5 Recce Regts remain as the country's Special Forces.

Recruitment in Angola: 32 Battalion

In August 1975, nearly three years after he had established the first Recce Commando, Breytenbach was dispatched to southern Angola to raise a unit from among troops loyal to Daniel Chipenda, who had recently defected to Holden Roberto's FNLA from Agostinho Neto's MPLA. This led to the formation of 'Battle Group Bravo', which would join 'Battle Group Alpha' (another indigenous force under South African command) as part of 'Zulu Force' – which was in action from the early stages of Operation 'Savannah' in October 1975. (One of the tasks of the SADF during 'Savannah' was to

D ANGOLA, COMOROS & SURINAME

(1) Costas Georgiou, alias 'Colonel Callan'; Angola, 1975–76

After arriving in Angola in 1975, this ex-British Parachute Regiment soldier of Greek-Cypriot descent took the *nom de guerre* 'Tony Callan'. As the leader of a predominantly British group of mercenaries in support of the pro-Western FNLA, 'Callan' (whose pseudonym recalled the hero of a popular British TV series) would have had priority of choice among the mixture of equipment and weapons provided. Photos show him wearing olive drab shirt and trousers with high-leg boots. His belt order includes a US-style canteen and carrier, a combat knife, and a utility pouch worn on his right. He has an unidentified shoulder rig for a handgun, and is holding an M1/M2 carbine fitted with a 30-round magazine. The M1 (semi-automatic) and M2 (fully automatic) fire a short .30cal carbine cartridge (7.62 x 33mm); while light, handy weapons, they are therefore largely ineffective beyond short ranges.

(2) Bob Denard; Kandani, Grande Comore, 1995

In September 1995, mercenaries under the 66-year-old Denard took control of Grande Comore, the main island of this small group in the western Indian Ocean. It was at least the third such operation that the veteran French mercenary had led there, and he had enjoyed power and wealth on Grande Comore during 1978–89. This time he had misjudged the

priorities of the previously-indulgent French intelligence services, and within days Denard and his men were forced to surrender to a French intervention force. He was photographed on 5 October 1995 at the end of his long career, moments before being taken into French custody. Note the elephant-hair bracelet on his right wrist, a reminder of his long association with Africa. (Notes on Denard's earlier career, and images of him in the Congo in 1962 and 1967, will be found in Men-at-Arms 492, *Modern African Wars (4): The Congo 1960–2002*, Plate C2 and pages 20 & 45.)

(3) Alan Boydell, SNAL Jungle Commando; Moengo, Suriname, 1989

A former Royal Marine, Englishman Alan Boydell has a long career in soldiering and as a private security contractor. In 1989 he joined a number of ex-servicemen in Suriname to instruct indigenous rebels of the so-called Jungle Commando. The green beret with bronze 'globe-and-buster' badge recalls his previous service. The camouflage-pattern shirt and the jungle boots are US Army surplus, and the trousers are British Army 'lightweights'. A British 58 Pattern belt supports an unidentified ammunition pouch and a canteen, and the weapon is a locally-purchased 12-gauge Mossburg pump-action shotgun. Boydell would later fight for both Croatian and Bosnian-Muslim forces in former Yugoslavia in the early 1990s – see Plate F3.

reorganize disaffected Angolan soldiers recruited to the anti-FAPLA cause.) 'Battle Group Bravo' was subsequently reinforced with an additional two companies, and detached to fight alongside 'Battle Group Foxbat', which had been formed mainly from ex-UNITA fighters.

Breytenbach intended to employ Bravo Group, as it came to be known, in a specialist counter-insurgency role, to track and destroy guerrilla units in their own base areas. In 1976, Bravo Group was officially recognized as part of the SADF and redesignated 32 Battalion, while Alpha Group was retitled 31 Battalion.

32 (Buffalo) Battalion was based at Omauni in South West Africa, from where foot patrols could readily deploy into southern Angola, where PLAN had established a number of bases. PLAN was supported by FAPLA, and both these organizations would become legitimate targets during SADF operations. As the war continued, PLAN evolved from a guerrilla force into a semi-conventional army, and 32 Bn adapted its tactics accordingly, operating in battalion strength when necessary. In time the battalion's role was extended. Its men might be deployed as motorized infantry with heavy support weapons, as company-size search and destroy teams, or as airborne assault troops. In addition, 32 Bn's Reconnaissance Wing carried out various tasks, including ambushes, deep inside Angola.

In the early 1980s, a typical deployment might involve a company insertion either by helicopter or on foot. After establishing a temporary base (TB), operators would undertake reconnaissance or fighting patrols, as tasked. The TB location was changed as the unit scoured its area of operations (AO). Besides his personal weapon and ammunition, each man had a Bergen with several days' provisions. Deployments might continue for up to six weeks, with helicopters providing resupply and, if necessary, casualty evacuation.

Typically, platoons worked a rotating shift, with half the men on patrol while the other half rested. Following 'spoor' (tracks) across flat and all but featureless terrain, patrols regularly encountered enemy forces. This invariably resulted in a 'punch-up', which might be followed by days of activity as each side attempted to ambush the other. Depending on the

Pathfinder Company, 44 Para Bde was equipped with two Toyota Land Cruisers so radically modified as to be almost unrecognizable. This vehicle was equipped with two .50cal HMGs, and the other with a 20mm cannon. The company also had three Land Rovers, each with twin rear-mounted FN MAGs and a third for the commander; and three 2.5-ton Mercedes Unimogs carrying extra fuel and provisions, each also fitted with a machine gun. All vehicles had smoke dischargers, winches, and foam-filled tyres. VHF radios were provided for internal use; section commanders also had HF sets for communication with base camp. In this photo, the Land Cruiser is crewed by two Rhodesians, a New Zealander and an American. (Gordon Brindley)

situation, reinforcements could be flown in to assist, while sizeable and more difficult targets were left for mechanized forces. Such was 32 Bn's ferocity in action that it would earn the grudging respect of the enemy, who gave it the Portuguese sobriquet *Os Terríveis* – 'The Terrible Ones'.

Negotiations for a settlement led to South Africa withdrawing its forces from Angola in August 1988. The following year, in November 1989, elections in South West Africa (renamed Namibia) resulted in a majority vote for SWAPO. With the end of South Africa's border war there was no longer a role for 32 Battalion. After being retired to a new base at Pomfret – a squalid little town, the site of a disused asbestos mine on the edge of the Kalahari Desert – the unit was disbanded in 1993.

Directorate Special Tasks (DST) was a sub-unit of South African Military Intelligence Division. Among those recruited by DST for secret operations in Zimbabwe were former Rhodesians and, it is thought, ex-ZIPRA guerrillas. During a clandestine mission in August 1981 several men lost their lives, among them Dave Berry (centre), formerly of the Rhodesian SAS. (Private collection)

Pathfinders

In 1979, Col Breytenbach, now commanding the SADF's 44 Parachute Brigade, developed a concept that would provide it with an independent force for unconventional operations in the border areas of South West Africa. At the time, 44 Para Bde comprised three battalions soon to be joined by a new sub-unit – Pathfinder Company.

This company was unique in that it was made up almost entirely of ex-Rhodesian security forces personnel. Potential candidates had to pass a rigorous selection devised by the South African company commander, Capt Piet Botes, and CSM Peter McAleese (who had served in the Rhodesian SAS and BSAP since leaving Angola – see above, 'Colonel Callan'). 'Pre-selection' prepared aspiring applicants to attain the high level of fitness necessary to undergo selection.

Selection would vary from one intake to the next, but typically included a load-carry for about 105 miles (170km) over several days in the Drakensberg Mountains. During the first phase, lasting two days, candidates carried – in addition to their weapon, backpack and full fighting order – an 82lb (37kg) ammunition box. The second phase, undertaken without the ammo box, involved a 4-mile (6km) run with weapon and equipment, during which they were harassed by directing staff. Men who made it that far were asked if they wished to continue; those who were prepared to keep going would then be told that they had passed.

In January 1981, the Pathfinders were attached to C Coy, 1st Para Bn for Operation 'Vasbyt 5', an attack made in conjunction with 31 and 32 Bns against SWAPO and FAPLA positions near the Angolan town of Cuamato. Soon afterwards the company deployed on its first mobile task, providing close fire support during a 32 Bn assault against a SWAPO base. Subsequently, the company was deployed mainly on long-range vehicle and foot patrols, and in August it joined other units for Operation 'Protea', targeting SWAPO bases in Angola. In November 1981 the Pathfinders were parachuted into Angola during Operation 'Daisy', forming part of an assault force tasked with the destruction of PLAN headquarters at Bambi and a base at Cheraquera.

This was to be their last major operation. Not long afterwards Col Breytenbach was posted to a new command, and with him went any hope of the independent Pathfinder Company's continued existence. In January 1982 the company was disbanded, with those who had not yet completed their service being absorbed by the Recce Wing of 32 Battalion. During its short history Pathfinder Company had achieved much, at a cost of only one fatality (an Englishman, Steve Hadlow), and several others seriously wounded.

THE INDIAN OCEAN

THE COMOROS

Background

The Comoros archipelago, situated between Mozambique and northern Madagascar, had been partly a French possession since the late 19th century, and a protectorate since 1912. Its modest population inhabited four main islands: Grande Comore (Ngazidja), Mayotte (Mahoré), Anjouan (Nzwani), and Mohéli (Mwali).

In July 1975, President Ahmed Abdallah Abderemane upset the client relationship with France by announcing a unilateral declaration of independence, and granting autonomy to the different islands. France's President Valéry Giscard d'Estaing was placed in an awkward position, which was further complicated when Mayotte opted to remain under French rule as an overseas *département*. Before long, Abdallah Abderemane was ousted in a bloodless coup. Said Mohammed Djaffer took over as interim-president, but in the background Ali Soilih, the central figure behind the coup, discreetly maintained control.

Abdallah Abderemane fled from the capital – Moroni, on Grande Comore – to Anjouan. There he continued to pose a threat to the ruling party until September 1975, when Congo veteran Bob Denard orchestrated his arrest and subsequent exile. Ali Soilih emerged as the islands' new leader. He severed all ties with France, and dispensed with the region's more puritanical Islamic traditions, but by 1978 his popularity had dwindled, and increasing tension led to rioting and deaths on Grande Comore.

Bob Denard, meanwhile, had not been idle. He was probably involved in Angola, and in January 1977 he led an abortive coup in Benin, West Africa. He was then offered a contract to depose the same man he had helped install two years previously, and to replace him with none other than Ahmed Abdallah Abderemane. The operation was probably sanctioned, and at least partially funded, by the French external intelligence service.

The 1978 coup

In May 1978 the trawler *Antinea* arrived off the Comoros, carrying Denard and some 50 mercenaries. During the night of 12/13 May they clambered into three Zodiac inflatables, and, after a rough passage in choppy water, beached at Itsandra on the west coast of Grande Comore. The mercenaries, wearing black fatigues and with faces darkened with camouflage cream, were only lightly armed with pump-action shotguns, hunting rifles and diving knives; they would seize military weapons from

Chad, mid-1982: Bruno de la Chapelle, a.k.a. 'Rio', was one of three French mercenaries sent by Bob Denard to work with Hissène Habré's FAN. He is seen here repairing a vehicle-mounted BM-16 multiple rocket launcher shortly before FAN's advance on the capital, N'djamena. Rio was killed in a training accident in the Comoros in 1983. (Hugues de Tappie)

Comorian forces as the operation developed. Communications were provided by hand-held radios.

After establishing a beachhead, they cut nearby telephone lines; some were deployed to secure the area, while the remainder headed inland. Two teams had been tasked with seizing military camps at Kandani and Voidjou. The former was just east of Itsandra beach, and the other several kilometres away between Moroni and the international airport. Both objectives were taken with a minimum of fuss. The majority of the team continued to Moroni, linking up with their comrades there and taking control of the radio station on the city outskirts. Ali Soilih was apprehended at the Presidency; political prisoners were freed from the jail, and within hours it was over. Denard and his men were in control of Grande Comore; no more than ten Comorians had been killed, and one mercenary injured.

An interim 'politico-military directorate' was formed by Denard, Abdallah Mohammed (soon to be prime minister) and Abbas Djoussouf (the future defence minister). A new government took office, with Ahmed Abdallah Abderemane and another of the coup instigators, Mohammed Ahmed, as co-presidents. Days later Ali Soilih was dead, killed by a person or persons unknown. Denard remained on the directorate for two months, before resigning in order to concentrate on his responsibilities as head of the 500–man Presidential Guard and the security apparatus. By that time Ali Soilih's small Comorian army had been replaced by a new force, trained and led by mercenaries.

Under pressure from France, Denard agreed to reduce his force to between 15 and 20 military advisers. Later in 1978 a new arrival, 'Commandant Charles' (probably a Belgian, Roger Ghys), took over as army commander and military adviser to Abdallah Abderemane, who assumed sole presidential power in December. Denard retained command of the Presidential Guard, and exercised considerable power in the background. Taking a local wife, he converted to Islam, and settled at Daché north of Moroni. Over the next ten years he became wealthy from a range of business interests, and is thought also to have profited from cooperating with the French government.

Interlude in Chad, 1981–90

Before long, another war would beckon. Chad had been granted independence from France on 11 August 1960. In a desperately poor country chronically divided by religious and ethnic differences, it was inevitable that civil war would follow. Following independence Chad maintained links with France, which would retain a watchful military presence in the country for the best part of two decades.

At about the end of 1981, Denard was approached to assist the pro-French Hissène Habré, commander of the Armed Forces of the North *(Forces armées du nord* – FAN). Denard sent a small team to Chad, with instructions to help reorganize and train Habré's forces, using equipment and weapons seized from the Libyan-supported forces of the Transitional Government of National Unity *(Gouvernement d'union nationale de transition* – GUNT). Of the three mercenaries involved, one was killed in action in Chad, and another died later in a shooting accident in the Comoros.

In October 1982, Habré was inaugurated as president and a new government was formed. More of Denard's mercenaries arrived in Chad to assist Habré. In 1983 (Operation 'Manta'), and again in 1986 (Op 'Épervier'), France committed regular combat forces to support the government. With this French assistance and American aid, Habré's forces went on to conduct a notably successful campaign against incursion by Libyan regular troops; he would retain his hold on the country until November 1990, when he was deposed by his military commander Idriss Déby.

The coups of 1989 and 1995

In the meantime, the Comoros had experienced yet another change of government. Towards the end of November 1989, Abdallah Abderemane was shot dead under disputed circumstances, and Said Mohammed Djohar was installed as interim president. Denard, a prime suspect, departed with his fellow mercenaries the following month.

For nearly six years Denard maintained a relatively low profile, though attracting media attention in 1993 when he stood trial in France for his involvement in Benin 16 years previously; he was handed a five-year suspended

---

E

COLOMBIA & SIERRA LEONE

(1) Colombia mercenary; Operation 'Phoenix', 1989
One of the former servicemen recruited by Peter McAleese, this mercenary prepares for the attempt to assassinate the Colombian 'drug baron' Pablo Escobar. He is wearing Colombian Army camouflage uniform, and a balaclava with a fluorescent yellow cross for overhead identification from the helicopters which were to land the party. His weapon is a 5.56mm Colt AR-15, the commercial version of the M16, fitted with an improvised para-cord sling. The tactical vest was custom-made to accommodate whatever equipment was needed, including additional magazines, a radio, handgun and grenades. The men's civilian clothes and 'shock packs' with escape clothing, cash, etc., were carried in an attached small back-pack.

(2) South African contractor, Executive Outcomes; Sierra Leone, c. 1995
Executive Outcomes was a 'private military company' in the truest sense, noted for its combat-experienced personnel, and for providing the necessary logistics and equipment. In the field, the similarity of appearance between EO and 32 Bn SADF was no coincidence: Eeben Barlow, the South African founder of EO, had served in that unit, as had many EO operators. The camouflage pattern of the shirt and trousers seems to resemble that of 32 Bn, while company-issue load-bearing equipment, as worn by this former member of SADF special forces, evolved from variations tested during the Rhodesian and South African bush wars. Personal weapons tended to be of the AK family.

(3) Angolan contractor, Executive Outcomes; Sierra Leone, c. 1995
A good number of EO contractors were black Africans, who offered a wealth of experience gained in fighting for the SADF in the 1980s. This Angolan soldier had served in both 4 and 5 Recce Regts as well as 32 Bn, before retiring as a senior NCO and joining EO. Here he wears a mixture of military and civilian clothing.

Hugues de Tappie (centre) also worked with Bob Denard in the Comoros before joining a training team in Chad, of which he is the only survivor. This photo was taken at Massaguet, shortly before the capture of N'djamena in mid-1982. (Hugues de Tappie)

sentence. He next came to prominence when, during the night of 27/28 September 1995, he and a small force of mercenaries returned to Grande Comore in circumstances similar to the 1978 coup. They quickly secured their objectives and captured President Said Mohammed Djohar, who had been accused of misrule and misappropriation of government funds. There was only token resistance from the Comorian forces, several hundred of whom chose to side with the mercenaries.

However, just days later, on 4 October, France sent a military intervention force to suppress his coup, and Denard and his mercenary-led force surrendered without resistance. Djohar was replaced as interim president by the moderate Caabi el-Yachroutu Muhammad, until the election of President Mohammed Taki Abdoulkarim in March 1996.

After lengthy detention on remand in France, Denard was put on trial in 2006–07, and eventually received a (largely suspended) prison sentence. By then afflicted with Alzheimer's disease, he was spared further confinement, and died in France in October 2007 at the age of 78.

THE SEYCHELLES

Background
The Seychelles is a widely scattered group of more than 100 small islands situated in the Indian Ocean. The capital, Victoria, is located on the main island of Mahé, some 650 miles (1,050km) north-east of Madagascar, which in 1981 was home for the majority of the Comoros population of about 67,000. The Seychelles is known as a 'tropical paradise', and its economy depends almost entirely upon tourism.

In 1976, Britain's Labour government imposed (largely unwelcome) independence on this crown colony. The chief minister was James Mancham, whose pro-Western Seychelles Democratic Party had been elected six years previously, but Britain's terms for independence stipulated that a coalition government should take over. Accordingly, in 1976 Mancham reached an accommodation with the socialist France-Albert René, leader of the opposition Seychelles People's United Party. A year later, while Mancham was in London attending the Commonwealth Heads of Government Conference, René mounted a coup and declared himself president. He instituted a one-party state and, with the assistance of Tanzania's President Nyerere, established a small army.

Although René had permitted the United States to maintain a satellite tracking station on Mahé, he also allowed the Soviets to construct a military base on Coetivy, 165 miles (270km) to the south-west. Any cooperation with the USSR was perceived as a threat by South Africa. By November 1981, the now 62-year-old former Congo mercenary Mike Hoare had been entrusted with carrying out a coup with the tacit approval of the governments of both South Africa and Kenya, with the intention of re-installing 'Jimmy' Mancham. South Africa would supply a mercenary force with arms and ammunition captured by the SADF in Angola. Kenyan troops were to be placed on readiness to assume control of the Seychelles immediately after the takeover. As preparations got underway, Mancham began to lose enthusiasm; another prominent Seychellois, Gérard Hoarau, was therefore selected to become 'vice-president elect' preparatory to being installed as leader of a new government.

Hoare, sometimes accompanied by other ex-Congo veterans, conducted three reconnaissance missions to Mahé. However, the majority of his force would be recruited from among former members of the Rhodesian security forces, and volunteers from 2 Recce Cdo, the CF reservist special forces unit of the SADF.

Operation 'Anvil', 1981: the plan

The mercenaries were to arrive at Mahé airport posing as a drinking club, 'The Ancient Order of Frothblowers'. They would comprise three main groups, to be preceded by an advance party of three two-man teams, each of which was to conduct target recces and, if necessary, provide protection for the main force on its arrival. Arms and ammunition would be provided on the island.

Group 1, commanded by Barney Carey, comprised ten men (including an advance party), and was to neutralize the army barracks at Union Vale just north of Victoria, before taking over the nearby radio station.

Group 2 comprised 20 or so mostly ex-Rhodesian operators, led by Mike Webb with Rich Stannard as second-in-command. One 12-man section under Peter Hean was to take the main army barracks at Pointe La Rue at the southern end of the airport runway. Simon Willar and three other men were to clear buildings housing Tanzanian military advisers, situated between the barracks and the airport terminal. The control tower was to be taken over by Charles Goatley and Vernon Prinsloo.

Group 3, comprising about 18 predominantly 2 Recce Cdo personnel under ex-Congo mercenary Tullio Moneta, seconded by Pieter Dooreward, were responsible for targets in Victoria itself: Army Headquarters, State House, and the Presidential Palace.

Mike Hoare's four-man headquarters was to establish itself in the Cable & Wireless offices near State House. Jerry Puren had been tasked with distracting Bob Noddyn, an old friend from their Congo days and latterly the training officer of the Presidential Guard. A secondary objective seems to have been the Russian embassy; Martin Dolinchek and yet another Congo veteran, Peter Duffy, were apparently going to gain entry and photograph

The Comoros, October 1995: Bob Denard (standing) and a member of his mercenary-led force shortly before surrendering to the French military at Kandani on 5 October – see Plate D2. This concluded both Denard's long association with the Comoros, and his 34-year mercenary career. (Anne Nosten/Gamma-Rapho via Getty Images)

whatever documents might have been of interest to South Africa's National Intelligence Service. (Dolinchek, who appears to have taken leave from the NIS in order to join the Seychelles operation, had been sent to Mahé early on, as had Hoare's brother-in-law Bob Sims, who had been tasked with setting up a safe house in Victoria.)

Success would be dependent on achieving total surprise. Once the key locations were under their control, the mercenaries were to await the arrival of the Kenyan back-up force, whereupon they would revert to being 'tourists' before returning to South Africa, each $11,000 richer.

The operation

When the advance party gathered to fly to Mahé over 21–22 November, a major flaw in the operation was revealed: none of the promised arms and ammunition had been delivered to the island. Instead, the men's personal weapons, plus just two full magazines apiece, had been concealed in the bottom of each of their holdalls. In the event, the advance party passed through Customs with ease (the airport X-ray machines had apparently been switched off), but this sudden change of plans would ultimately be the undoing of Mike Hoare's 'last hurrah'.

On the morning of Wednesday 25 November, weapons were issued to the main mercenary force (at which point one man wisely took the opportunity to withdraw). The remainder were taken by road across the

F FORMER YUGOSLAVIA
(1) Volunteer, Croatian Army; Vinkovci, 1991
This 19-year-old British volunteer had virtually no prior military experience, and little idea as to what he would do when he arrived in Yugoslavia. Bemused officials directed the politically naïve teenager to Vinkovci in eastern Croatia, facing the Serbian Vojvodina front, where he joined a unit of the newly formed Croatian Army (HV). In the early stage of the wars in Yugoslavia military forces used whatever clothing and equipment were available. In this case, a so-called 'tiger-stripe' camouflage jacket resembling that of the Yugoslav National Army (JNA) Military Police is worn over a Norwegian-style zipped sweater, while the combat trousers may be US surplus M1982 Woodland pattern or the Croatian-made copy. The field cap bears the HV's badge of the Croatian red-and-white checkered shield within a crowned gold border. The weapon is a 7.62mm Zastava M70B1, the standard Yugoslavian service rifle.

(2) 'Fran', Croatian Army 110th Brigade; Karlovac, 1991
In late 1991 this French former national-service paratrooper was a volunteer serving in the Croatian 110th Bde at Karlovac in north-central Croatia, facing the Serb Banija enclave to the south; the following year he served in Bosnia with the Frankopan Battalion. He too is shown with the kind of assorted clothing and equipment typical of the early campaigns. The HV badge is pinned to a British Army cap in Disruptive Pattern Material (DPM), which Fran acquired from a British comrade. The sleeveless jerkin and the trousers are locally made, in a faded pattern resembling US M1982 Woodland; the jerkin is similar but not identical to one issued to JNA paratroops. The Norwegian-style sweater and the boots are probably West German. A US web belt is supported by a yoke of unknown origin. The box-like carrier at his right front holds a JNA mess

kit, comprising a plastic 1-litre water bottle and cup, plastic food container, messtin, knife, fork and spoon. Hidden on his left side is an ex-Romanian Army pouch set holding three AK magazines and a Yugoslav hand grenade. Again, the weapon is the M70B1 rifle; the bayonet (attached to his left yoke harness) could be used in conjunction with its scabbard as wire cutters. The strictly non-regulation neck scarf is a lady's stocking.

After Bosnia, Fran worked as an instructor for militiamen in the Comoros: 'holidays for me', as he described it. Much later still, he would fight against *Daesh* (ISIS) with Kurdish forces in Syria – see Plate H3.

(3) Alan Boydell, HVO Baja Kraljevic Anti-Terrorist Group; Mostar, 1992
This former Royal Marine and Suriname mercenary (see also Plate D3) first arrived in the Balkans in 1991. He initially joined the Croatian forces, which were at that stage being favourably reported in the Western media. After recovering from a mortar-bomb wound, Boydell subsequently fought in Bosnia-Herzegovina. He is illustrated here during the 1992 siege of Mostar on the Dalmatian front, where he was posted to a Bosnian-Croat 'special police anti-terrorist unit' led by one Mladen Naletilić (alias 'Tuta') He wears a British Army DPM windproof smock and tropical trousers, and is armed with a folding-stock AK-74: 'an excellent weapon'. Subsequently, Boydell switched sides, and served with Bosnian-Muslim forces in besieged Sarajevo for the rest of the war. (Naletilić called his unit the Convicts Bn – *Bojna Kažnjenička*; already convicted for the murder of a fellow Croatian policeman, he would subsequently be sentenced by the International Criminal Tribunal for the former Yugoslavia (ICTY) in The Hague to 20 years' imprisonment for war crimes.)

The Seychelles, late 1981: mercenaries Aubrey Brooks (left) and Roger England, slightly the worse for wear after being captured following Mike Hoare's failed coup attempt. This photo shows the pair when they and their fellow mercenaries were first paraded in front of the international media. Brooks and England were among those initially sentenced to death, but released some 18 months later. (Aubrey Brooks)

South African border to Matsapa airport in Swaziland, where they boarded a Royal Swazi Airlines flight for Mahé.

On arrival, nearly everybody had cleared Customs when, for reasons that are still not entirely clear, Johan Fritz (2 Recce) was stopped and searched. His concealed AK was discovered. An American mercenary, Barry Gribbin, hastily made ready his own weapon and opened fire, wounding an official and at the same time accidentally killing Fritz.

Mike Hoare had no option but to commence the operation there and then. Taking advantage of the confusion, Bob Sims and Martin Dolinchek of the greeting party left the airport, while the remaining men prepared for imminent action.

Aubrey Brooks, Ken Dalgliesh, Roger England and Charlie Dukes were ordered to drive to Pointe La Rue to prevent troops there from deploying. At the barracks, they parked their car outside the entrance barrier; their intention was to take the guardroom without any shooting, to avoid alerting the entire camp. However, one of three soldiers on duty opened fire, wounding Brooks in the leg and Dukes in the arm. Soon afterwards, a 12.7mm heavy machine gun opened up from inside the camp, and the four mercenaries were compelled to withdraw to nearby high ground.

From there, they observed the arrival of Hoare with others of the main party; there had been no time to distribute hand-held radios, so neither group was able to communicate with the other. An effort was made to bring fire on to the 12.7mm MG, but the men's AKs had had their butts removed to aid concealment; consequently they were difficult to aim, and inaccurate at anything over short range. Furthermore, the wounded Brooks was going into shock. He was advised to make his way downhill to join Hoare; England, Dukes and Dalgliesh followed, but when they arrived Brooks was nowhere to be seen. Dense vegetation and approaching darkness made it impossible to carry out a thorough search (Brooks was later captured). A joint decision was made for the whole party to withdraw to the airport, to return and deal with the barracks in the morning.

Things were no better at the airport. There, a BRDM armoured vehicle had been immobilized and its driver killed (he was to be the only Seychellois fatality). But Hoare had lost the initiative, and it was clear that the operation had no hope of success. The mercenaries were saved by the arrival at Mahé of an Air India Boeing. The airliner was hijacked, and its pilot was forced to fly to South Africa, together with his bewildered passengers and most of Hoare's men.

Aftermath

Those left behind in the Seychelles were all arrested and duly put on trial. Roger England, Barney Carey, Aubrey Brooks and Jerry Puren were sentenced to death, and Bob Sims and Martin Dolinchek received prison sentences of 10 and 20 years respectively. In the event, no one was executed, and all six were released in July 1983.

Mike Hoare and the remaining mercenaries were charged in South Africa under the 1972 Civil Aviation Offences Act. For hijacking the airliner, Hoare was sentenced to 10 years' imprisonment; other sentences ranged from 5 years down to (for the majority) 6 months. Charges were dropped against two men in return for their turning state's witness, and Charlie Dukes, who had been incapacitated at the time of the hijack, was acquitted. By mid-May 1984 nearly all had been released, and Mike Hoare walked free a year later.

Gérard Hoarau, who had been tipped to become president of the Seychelles had the coup succeeded, was assassinated in London by an unidentified gunman on 28 November 1985. France-Albert René continued to rule the Seychelles until obliged to step down in favour of Vice-President James Michel in April 2004; under a third leader, their regime was finally defeated in elections in 2020. Mike Hoare enjoyed a quiet retirement, initially in the South of France and later in South Africa, where he died in February 2020 at the age of 100.

SOUTH AMERICA

SURINAME

Background
Suriname, a Dutch colony since the early 19th century, lies on the north-eastern coast of South America between Guyana and French Guiana. It was developed as a major exporter of bauxite, some of the mines being located at Moengo in the north-east. Ethnically, the Surinamese include Hindustanis and Creoles, together with Javanese and a minority of Chinese, all descended from arrivals in the late 19th and early 20th centuries. About 10 per cent are Maroons or 'bush negroes', descended from escaped slaves, and Amerindians and Europeans make up small percentages.

Suriname became independent on 25 November 1975. After a turbulent few years, the democratically-elected government of Prime Minister Henck Aaron was overthrown in a military coup led by Desiré Bouterse, and replaced with President Johan Ferrier. A few months later, in August 1980, Bouterse deposed Ferrier, replacing him with Henk Chin A Sen; and in February 1982, Bouterse himself finally seized power.

Bouterse forged ties with Grenada's Marxist Prime Minister Maurice Bishop, and with Fidel Castro of Cuba. Reportedly, he also received financial aid from President Muammar Gaddafi in return for allowing Libya to establish a 'cultural mission' in Suriname's capital, Paramaribo, and both the Cubans and their Soviet allies were permitted to open embassies there. By 1984 Cubans and Libyans were allegedly involved in running a terrorist training camp near Sipaliwini, on the southern border with Brazil.

Mercenary involvement, 1986–91
In July 1986, a military post at Stolkertsijver was attacked by men loyal to one of Bouterse's former bodyguards, Ronnie Brunswijk. In a worsening crisis, small teams of mercenaries arrived to train and lead Brunswijk's Suriname National Liberation Army (SNLA), or 'Jungle Commando'. Bouterse is also rumoured to have employed mercenaries, in addition to receiving Cuban

Suriname, 1989: mercenaries at 'The Tasty Bite', a bar in Moengo, which they renamed 'The Nasty Bite'. (Left to right) Neil Finnighan, John Richards, Bill Oakey, Alan Boydell, Mick Pemberton and Oyvind Pedersen. Finnighan and Boydell had served in the Royal Marines, the others in the French Foreign Legion – thus their preference for wearing their green berets pulled either right or left. Jungle Commando patches can be seen on the shirtsleeves. (Private collection)

and Libyan military assistance. After three years of internal strife, Brunswijk and the then-President Ramsewak Shankar signed a peace accord in July 1989, but Bouterse, who still wielded actual control, vowed that there would be no compromise with the rebels.

In late 1989, while working on the London security 'circuit', former Royal Marine Alan Boydell was introduced to ex-French Foreign Légionnaire John Richards, and was recruited to help train Hindustani guerrillas of the SNLA in Suriname's north-western district of Nickerie. He was joined by Neil 'Finny' Finnighan (also ex-Royal Marines), Pat Baker (ex-Queen's Royal Irish Hussars), and former Légionnaires Oyvind Pedersen from Norway, Mick Pemberton from the UK, and Irishman Bill Oakey. Soon afterwards this group, accompanied by two French film-makers, departed for French Guiana.

On arrival, the mercenaries equipped themselves with locally-purchased shotguns before beginning an arduous trek to Moengo, which had been captured by the SNLA the previous year. Before long the Frenchmen, becoming increasingly nervous, cut short their assignment and left, as did Baker, who had been struggling to keep up. The remainder carried on, but along the way increasing friction resulted in two distinct groups emerging: Richards, Pemberton and Pedersen formed one clique, and Boydell, Finnighan and Oakey the other.

At Moengo's Jungle Commando headquarters the mercenaries were welcomed by Ronnie Brunswijk. He was by then negotiating with the government, and there had been a change of plans. The mercenaries would not be working with Hindustanis as expected; they would instead instruct the Maroons of the Jungle Commando, who were engaged in an ongoing conflict with the minority Tucajana Amerindians. The Maroons were armed with badly neglected FALs, but after instruction in the importance of basic weapon care, training proper commenced. During this time a replacement for Pat Baker arrived: Gary Butts, another British former Légionnaire, who was immediately accepted into Richards' group.

Boydell's team was presented with an opportunity to assess the effectiveness of their training when they led a fighting patrol to a village that had been occupied by Tucajanas. After positioning themselves on nearby high ground the patrol initiated contact, whereupon the Maroons disappeared back into the bush, leaving Boydell, Finnighan and Oakey to face the Tucajanas' return fire. The trio made a hasty withdrawal.

For their part, the ex-Legion faction were tasked by Brunswijk to assassinate a Tucajana leader, 'Commander Thomas', whose base was in the south of the country. Instead, and to the chagrin of Brunswijk, the ex-Légionnaires attacked an army outpost, killing several soldiers. Boydell, Finnighan and Oakey were ordered to report to Brunswijk for questioning, during which all three made every effort to distance themselves from Richards. Evidently Brunswijk was satisfied that at least three of his mercenaries did not represent any kind of threat; allegedly, he then disclosed that during secretly recorded telephone calls, Pemberton had announced his intention to murder Boydell and his two friends (which Pemberton later denied). It was also claimed that Richards had deposited the men's pay in a personal bank account. Furthermore, Dutch and French intelligence agencies were said to have informed Brunswijk that Richards was planning his assassination. Only those who were present know what was discussed, but the outcome would be fatal.

After arriving back at Moengo, the ex-Légionnaires were seized and interrogated. Pedersen, Pemberton and Butts were allowed to leave Suriname, but John Richards was taken into the jungle and executed. Boydell and his two comrades were free to resume training duties, and in time all would return home. Of the three, Alan Boydell would continue to ply his trade: he was soon back in uniform, this time in Yugoslavia (see below).

COLOMBIA

Background

Colombia's politics are intimately entwined with the country's illegal but immensely lucrative narcotics industry. The situation has created so-called 'drug barons' who preside over their own fiefs, protected by their own private armies. Among the more influential figures in the Colombian underworld during the mid-1980s were the rivals José Gonzalo Rodríguez Gacha, alias *El Méjicano* ('The Mexican'), and Pablo Emilio Escobar Gaviria of the Medellín-based drug cartel.

Colombia's drug wars also attracted mercenaries. In 1988–89 an Israeli training team ran courses for the Association of Farmers and Ranchers of the Middle Magdalena (*Asociación Campesina de Ganaderos y Agricultores del Magdalena Medio* – ACDEGAM). This was a civic group that performed various community services, while at the same time providing a paramilitary force for Rodríguez Gacha.

In summer 1988, former Angola mercenaries Dave Tomkins and Peter McAleese were also in Colombia, discussing with government officials the possibility of attacking the headquarters of the Revolutionary Armed Forces of Colombia (*Fuerzas Armadas Revolucionarias de Colombia* – FARC). Supported by Cuba and funded primarily by the narcotics trade, FARC was responsible for a series of terrorist incidents in an ongoing campaign against the government. However, the political authorities had a complicated agenda; they were reluctant to resort to outright military action, preferring instead to pursue negotiations. Members of the Colombian security forces, frustrated by this approach, decided to find an alternative solution.

Colombia, Operation 'Phoenix', 1989: Dean Shelley (left) and Dave Tomkins enjoy a beer at their base. Shelley was a veteran of the Rhodesian Light Infantry, and both the SADF's 32 Bn and Pathfinder Company, 44 Para Brigade. Tomkins had been a mercenary with 'Colonel Callan' and Peter McAleese in Angola, and was subsequently involved in security work in Rhodesia. (Dave Tomkins)

Planned strike against FARC, 1988

The proposition was one that appealed to McAleese and Tomkins. After he had prepared a plan of attack, McAleese began recruiting nine men, all veterans of Rhodesia and/or South Africa. Tomkins organized logistics; in order not to attract official attention by depleting the military budget, it seems likely that Rodríguez Gacha agreed to provide the necessary funding.

By the third week in August 1988 all 11 mercenaries were in Colombia. They were taken 125 miles (200km) through the mountains of the eastern Cordillera to the river-port town of Puerto Boyacá, and from there across a lake to a small island known locally as Isla de la Fantasia (Fantasy Island), where they were accommodated in a villa. The men were issued with Heckler & Koch G3 rifles, and McAleese devised a training syllabus incorporating weapon-training, immediate-action drills, fire and movement, battle skills, patrolling, and navigation exercises.

During an impromptu visit, Rodríguez Gacha asked McAleese whether it was possible to assault the FARC secretariat at their main guerrilla base several miles from Casa Verde. McAleese thought so, but not with 11 men. Consequently, the team was joined by about 50 ACDEGAM trainees. As time passed, there was confusion as to the actual nature of the operation and when it might occur. After waiting in vain, McAleese requested that his men be allowed to return to Bogotá, where they were duly paid off and the team was disbanded. McAleese and Tomkins were the last to leave, on 18 November, four and a half months after first setting foot in Colombia.

Operation 'Phoenix', 1989: the plan

In February 1989, Dave Tomkins was again approached, but with an altogether different proposal: this time the target was the drug baron Pablo Escobar.

Tomkins and McAleese returned to Colombia to be briefed on the new task. Escobar owned a property between Puerto Triumpho and Medellín. This Hacienda Nápoles was set in a jungle clearing, surrounded by security fencing and guard towers, and defended by an estimated 80 men armed with M60 or FN general-purpose machine guns, AR-15 rifles, and Uzi and Ingram sub-machine guns. The objective of Operation 'Phoenix' was to attack Hacienda Nápoles as soon as intelligence could confirm Escobar's presence there, and to kill him.

This time Tomkins arranged the recruiting, leaving McAleese to focus on planning. Five of the original team returned to Colombia, accompanied by six new members. For security reasons, none of them had been informed of the new target; this caused Australian Terry Tangney (a veteran of the Rhodesian and South African bush wars) to withdraw from the mission. The remainder concentrated on training

Mercenaries rehearse prior to the 1989 attempt to assassinate the drug baron Pablo Escobar; directing events (far right) is Peter McAleese. After his SADF service, McAleese had been employed by a South African private security company. Although seriously injured in both a helicopter crash and a later parachuting accident, he continued to work internationally in the private security sector until his eventual retirement.

Operation 'Phoenix' would be very well equipped, with three helicopters and two fixed-wing aircraft; this Bell 204, with Colombian police markings, would be flown by an ex-officer of the Colombian Air Force. (Dave Tomkins)

and preparation. This time there was no shortage of equipment. The team were equipped with AR-15 and G3 rifles, 9mm handguns, grenades (including white phosphorous and coloured smoke), 66mm M72 light anti-tank rocket launchers (LAWs), and an abundance of ammunition. The former safe-breaker Tomkins was provided with whatever he needed to manufacture explosive devices.

The mercenaries were joined by 'Tiger', a police narcotics officer, and 'Toyco',

At La Guagua, Colombia, mercenaries relax between McAleese's thorough training sessions. Between them these men had experience in the Royal Marines, the SAS, the RLI, and SADF. (Dave Tomkins)

a former officer in the Colombian Air Force, who would pilot the assault team's two helicopters – a Hughes 500 and a Bell 204. As additional air support, there was a Cessna fixed-wing aircraft fitted with Telstar radio re-broadcasting equipment; a 12-seat Cessna Caravan to evacuate the force on completion; and a Bell 206 JetRanger helicopter, for use as back-up and in case of casualty evacuation.

Those in the support group were provided with G3 rifles, 9mm pistols, LAWs, and rifle and hand grenades. Everyone carried a personal radio with earpiece and microphone. Dress was Colombian camouflage uniforms, black balaclavas with a phosphorescent yellow cross on top for overhead identification, and custom-made tactical vests; McAleese had also acquired body armour. Each man was equipped with a 'shock pack' and escape kit, the latter including civilian clothes, a compass, and 300,000 *pesos* in cash.

Operation 'Phoenix' would be an airborne assault. The mercenaries were to overfly Hacienda Nápoles while McAleese, manning a pintle-mounted GPMG in the Hughes 500 piloted by 'Tiger', and supported by those in the Bell 204 flown by 'Toyco', opened fire on guard towers overlooking the target area. With any immediate threat thus neutralized, the Hughes would hover at roof-top height over the villa and gatehouse to enable Tomkins to drop satchel charges to kill or disable the occupants. The Hughes would then cover the deployment of the assault group and part of the support group by the Bell 204. As soon as the Bell was clear, the Hughes would come in to land the remaining three of the five-man support element, before orbiting the scene as McAleese's command helicopter and gunship.

The main task of the support group was to 'fire in' the assault group during their sweep through the hacienda, and to cover their withdrawal after it was confirmed that Escobar was dead. Finally, the mercenaries were to regroup at a designated LZ for helicopter extraction to a nearby airstrip, where they would transfer to the waiting Cessna Caravan.

The operation

On Saturday, 3 June 1989 word was received that Escobar was at the villa, and 'Phoenix' was initiated. The route took the helicopters over mountains, and during the flight the weather deteriorated without warning, reducing visibility. Disorientated, 'Tiger' attempted to clear a rise, but flew the Hughes 500 straight into trees and dense foliage. Had the helicopter impacted against rock there might well have been no survivors; in the event, the critically injured pilot was dead within minutes, and McAleese was badly hurt and unable to move unaided. Tomkins and two Colombians escaped serious injury. Radio contact was re-established with the Bell 204, and eventually all four survivors were evacuated. For official purposes, 'Tiger' was reported to have died during a classified police mission; his body was later recovered, and buried with honours.

Second and third contracts, 1989 and 1991

Undeterred, Dave Tomkins returned to the UK and recruited another four team members, including two helicopter pilots. All five arrived in Colombia on 5 July 1989. The operation might still have gone ahead, but six weeks later a series of murders, including that of Luis Carlos Galán, the country's leading presidential candidate, provoked tough government action against the suspected perpetrators. Escobar's known assets, including Hacienda Nápoles, were seized. In an effort to avoid capture the drug baron went into hiding, and in so doing unwittingly foiled any further assassination plans. Shortly afterwards, on 3 September, the mercenary team dispersed.

In June 1991, Colombia's President César Gaviria Trujillo promised to end the extradition of drug traffickers to the USA, and to impose only reduced prison sentences on any who surrendered. Escobar was among those who took advantage of the offer, and was held (in some comfort) in a secluded location in the hills overlooking his home town, Envigado, protected on the inside by six of his top lieutenants, and with external security provided by 40 guards.

Before long, Dave Tomkins was offered yet a third contract – this time to kill everyone being held at Envigado. A plan was devised by which a Cessna A-37 Dragonfly turbojet ground-attack aircraft would drop 8,000kg (nearly 17,650lbs) of explosives onto the target area, before an assault team stormed the building. Tasked with acquiring the aircraft, Tomkins located one in the United States, and for several months attempted to arrange its export – unaware that he was the victim of a Customs 'sting' operation. Tipped off in time, Tomkins was able to avoid arrest and returned to the UK. In July 1992, Escobar escaped from Envigado before he could be transferred to more secure and uncomfortable detention.

Aftermath

Rodríguez Gacha, principal financier of the original Operation 'Phoenix', was shot dead by Colombian police on 15 December 1989. Pablo Escobar was killed in a shoot-out with government forces four years later, on 2 December 1993.

Dave Tomkins, in the meantime, was indicted in the Southern District of Florida for conspiracy to violate the Arms Export Control Act in relation to the aircraft he had sourced there. In September 2003 Tomkins, now 63 years old, revisited the United States, unaware that there was an outstanding warrant for his arrest. He was detained on arrival at Houston's George Bush International Airport, was duly tried and convicted, and spent the next two and a half years inside six federal prisons. In March 2006, he was once more a free man – and working as a contractor in the Middle East.

THE BREAK-UP OF YUGOSLAVIA

Background

The Federal People's Republic of Yugoslavia was established at the end of World War II under the rule of the wartime Communist Partisan leader Marshal Josip Broz 'Tito'. While keeping the USSR at arm's length, his regime enforced an uneasy but functioning co-existence between the country's various historically hostile religious/ ethnic communities, which lasted for 36 years. After Tito's death in 1980, national tensions – particularly between traditionally Orthodox Christian Serbia and Catholic Croatia – began to challenge the federal government. (There is no space here to explain Yugoslavia's complex jigsaw-puzzle of ethnic blocs and isolated enclaves, but interested readers are directed to Osprey Elite 138, *The Yugoslav Wars (1): Slovenia and Croatia 1991–95*, and Elite 146, *The Yugoslav Wars (2): Bosnia, Kosovo and Macedonia 1992–2001*.)

By 1990 this unrest was being harnessed by several regional leaders. The most powerful was the Serbian Communist Party leader and Yugoslav President, Slobodan Milošević, who embraced the pre-World War II concept of a 'Greater Serbia'. Prominent among his opponents were the nationalist President Franjo Tuđman of Croatia, and the social democrat President Milan Kučan of Slovenia. On 25 June 1991 both Croatia and, separately, Slovenia declared their independence.

Outbreak of hostilities

Troops and armour of the Yugoslav National Army (*Jugoslovenska narodna armija* – JNA) were deployed in response; the JNA's rank-and-file were mixed, but its commanders were predominantly Serbian. Opposing the JNA

Croatia, December 1991, early in the disintegration of Yugoslavia: former French paratrooper 'Fran' photographed while serving with a small group of 'Internationals' in the Croatian Army's 110. karlovačka brigade. See Plate F2. (Private collection)

In late 1991 this 51-year-old Briton was the only foreign volunteer with a small group of the Croatian Party of Rights militia (*Hrvatske obrambene snage* – HOS) defending Mala Bosna, not far from Vinkovci on eastern Croatia's Vojvodina front. He is believed to have been in the Royal Green Jackets, before joining the Australian Army and serving in Vietnam. He was fatalistic about his prospects: 'I've got nothing else to do – Nothing to do, and the rest of my life to do it in.' (Private collection)

in Slovenia was a lightly armed but well organized and determined Territorial Force *(Teritorialna obramba – TO)*. JNA forces put up only token resistance, and within ten days the Slovenes had achieved their aim, at a cost of some 60 lives.

In Croatia the situation would be very different. Croatia's Territorial Force and new National Guard (*Zbor narodne garde* – ZNG) took over JNA barracks and depots, capturing large quantities of equipment including tanks, other armoured vehicles and heavy weapons. They quickly formed a Croatian Army (*Hrvatska vojska* – HV), which attracted many JNA deserters. This was soon supported by large militarized police forces under the Ministry of Internal Affairs (*Ministarstvo unutarnjih poslova* – MUP). These Croatian forces were confronted not only by the JNA but also by numerous ethnic-Serb militias within Croatia, particularly in the straggling Krajina region along the southern borders with Bosnia-Herzegovina.

Conventional warfare devastated towns and villages, their populations driven from their homes by mortar and artillery barrages, bombing, and tank and infantry assaults. In parallel, initial clashes between Serb and Croat militias became increasingly brutal. The armies of both sides dug in, as they attempted to consolidate what had been won.

By mid-1992 the first units of a United Nations Protection Force (UNPROFOR) had deployed to Croatia, but with only a limited remit. Fighting soon spread to neighbouring Bosnia-Herzegovina, where complex hostilities broke out between three distinct communities: Bosnian-Muslim, Bosnian-Serb, and Bosnian-Croat. This war continued for three and a half years; it was not until 21 November 1995 that international pressure led to the conclusion of the Dayton peace agreement, enforced by a NATO Implementation Force (IFOR). This brought to a (partial) end Europe's most protracted and bloody conflict since World War II.

Foreign fighters, 1991–95

After the outbreak of war in Croatia, initial foreign volunteers, some of them attracted by rumours of a non-existent 'International Brigade', began to arrive singly and in small groups. On arrival, they were usually integrated with Croatian units, initially of the ZNG and then the Army (HV); of the Interior Ministry police; or of the Croatian Defence Alliance militia (*Hrvatske obrambene snage* – HOS) of the extreme nationalist Croatian Party of Rights (*Hrvatska stranka prava* – HSP).

As it continued, the war would attract all kinds: idealists, professional soldiers, and adventurers with no military experience – even, it is said, thrill-seekers from Germany who visited for weekend killing sprees. The first foreign volunteer was probably Kaj, a former soldier in the Danish Army, who had been holidaying in Yugoslavia when Croatia declared independence. At first Kaj served the Croatians in an intelligence-gathering role, posing as an innocent tourist with his Danish-registered van. Later, he would serve as an ordinary foot soldier.

Croatia, February 1992: Keith Phillips (left), an instructor with a 'special police anti-terrorist unit' at the coastal town of Nin, near Zadar. He and the author had previously met in the 1970s, when both were serving in a Royal Marines. Phillips is sporting British parachute wings, a Royal Marines shoulder title, and a Union Jack patch. (Private collection)

Dave Fersen was an early British volunteer; formerly of the Royal Navy and latterly a deserter from the French Foreign Legion, he was given the local rank of lieutenant. Fersen was paid 16,000 *dinara* a month; others were fortunate if they received 11,000. The official exchange rate was then about 38 *dinara* to £1 sterling, so these figures equated to between £421 and £289 monthly – hardly the wages of a 'highly-paid mercenary' (volunteers found this term laughable). In any case, the local currency was soon greatly devalued, and became worthless outside the former Yugoslavia.

In Bosnia-Herzegovina, foreign fighters could be found on every side in the complex three-community struggle. Volunteers from Russia and Eastern Europe served with the Bosnian Serbs, while the Bosnian Muslims were joined by many (often unwelcome) *mujahideen* from all over the Muslim world. Westerners – some no doubt prompted by reports of the Bosnian-Serbs' siege of Sarajevo in 1993–95, and their massacre of Muslim civilians at Srebrenica in July 1995 – tended to join whoever was fighting against the Serbs.

Former Suriname mercenary Alan Boydell arrived in Croatia in October 1991, serving initially with the ZNG in Nuštar before joining the HV's 110th Bde in the Karlovac area. After being wounded he spent some time convalescing in the UK, before returning to serve in the HV's special-forces Frankopan Bn (*Bojna Frankopan*) in Bosnia-Herzegovina. Subsequently he made his way with several other foreign fighters to Mostar, serving under the Bosnian-Croat Croatian

Croatia, November 1992: former Royal Marine and Suriname mercenary Alan Boydell was also with the Croatian Army's 110th Karlovac Bde prior to joining the war in Bosnia-Herzegovina, where he eventually served with Bosnian-Muslim forces at Sarajevo. He is shown here at Lokve, wearing a British DPM cap and smock (see Plate F3), and test-firing a Browning .50cal HMG. (Private collection)

Defence Council (*Hrvatsko vijeće obrane* – HVO), which posted him to the Baja Kraljević Anti-Terrorist Group, led by Mladen Naletilić (alias 'Tuta'). The summary execution of four alleged '*četnici*' (a derogatory Croatian term for Serbs), actually innocent Bosnian Muslims, prompted Boydell to change sides to the Bosnian-Muslim army (ARBiH), serving in the Sarajevo area for the rest of the war.

The November 1995 Dayton peace agreement ended the wars in Croatia and Bosnia-Herzegovina, but not throughout the Balkans. In neighbouring Kosovo, hostilities broke out between Serbian Yugoslav forces and the Albanian-ethnic Kosovo Liberation Army (*Ushtria Çlirimtare e Kosovës* – UÇK). NATO intervened, sending warplanes to strike at Serbian forces in Kosovo before extending their range of targets across what remained of 'Greater Serbia'. On 9 June 1999, 11 weeks after the start of the air offensive, President Milošević was forced to accept NATO's peace terms, which included the withdrawal from Kosovo of all Serbian armed forces, special police and paramilitaries.

Aftermath

Slovenia, Croatia, Serbia, Montenegro, and North Macedonia have since been recognized as sovereign nations. Communal tensions remain high in a multi-ethnic federation in Bosnia-Herzegovina and also in Kosovo, where more limited forms of self-government were established, supported by the presence of small NATO and later European Union peacekeeping forces (STAFOR and EUFOR).

Among the main protagonists in the wars of 1991–95, Croatia's President Franjo Tuđman and Bosnia's wartime leader Alija Izetbegović died in 1999 and 2003 respectively. Between the mid-1990s and 2017 more than 200 suspected war criminals from all the belligerent groups would be extradited to

G **IRAQ**

(1) Security contractor, 2003–04

An increasing number of private security contractors signed up for high-risk work in the wake of the 2003 invasion of Iraq. The situation they found themselves in was at times quite disorganized: on arrival in-country they might be hurriedly deployed with little or no briefing, without body armour and with minimal and often inadequate equipment. Weapons, although easy to obtain, varied in quality. An early arrival in Iraq, this former Royal Welch Fusilier is wearing his own clothing and desert boots. AK rifles, seized from surrendered Iraqi forces, were standard issue. Spare magazines and extra rounds, passport, cash, etc, might be carried in a 'bug-out' bag, Communications were very basic, such as the hand-held Motorola radio shown here. Vehicles and their drivers were often hired locally.

(2) Ken 'Dusty' Duncan, security contractor, 2005

In time, things did get better, and by 2005 there was a distinct improvement in the kit and weapons of security contractors. New Zealander 'Dusty' Duncan was part of a small stand-alone team based at Al Mansour in Baghdad's so-called 'Red Zone'. The team operated with four armoured SUVs, some of them modified so that a gunner ('trunk monkey') could cover the rear. Available weapons for this purpose included a belt-fed 7.62mm PKM, and the illustrated 7.62mm RPK fitted with a drum magazine. It was uncomfortable riding in the back of such vehicles, with little headroom; Duncan brought his own rugby scrum-cap (shown under his left hand, on top of the spare RPK magazine). A 'bug-out bag' purchased from an American PX store is used as a floor cushion. Although there was no dress code for this particular team, Duncan's is fairly typical: under a civilian sleeveless 'fisherman's jacket', his Blackhawk tactical vest has a 9mm Glock 17 pistol tucked inside one of six pouches designed for M16/14 rifle magazines, but also accomodating those for AKs. Hanging round his neck is an identity-card holder, displaying his accreditation from the US Embassy in Baghdad as a Department of Defense contractor.

(3) Alan Boydell, security contractor, 2017

This very experienced ex-Royal Marine (see also Plates D3 & F3) first arrived in Iraq as a private security contractor in 2003. Fourteen years later he was operating in Mosul, escorting a British-American Explosive Ordnance Disposal team following up on Iraqi/US Coalition forces in their drive against Daesh. He is equipped with a UK Warrior Tactical Plate Carrier with four detachable twin 5.56mm pouches (suitable for AK magazines), and two auxiliary pouches. The olive-green pouch contains a Benchmade Safety Cutter Hook; attached next to it is a multitool; and his left-hand auxiliary pouch holds a Motorola radio, with a fist-mic carried across and fixed to his right shoulder brace. His weapon is a modified AK.

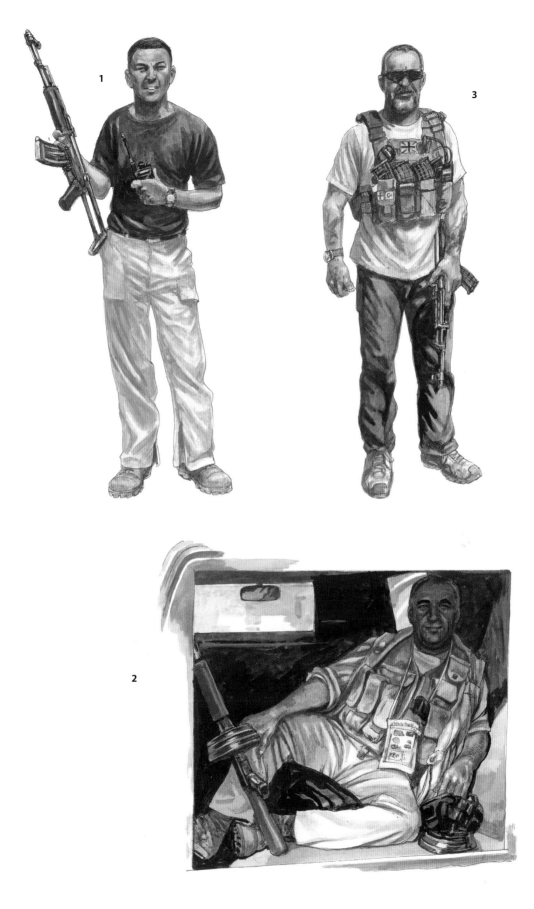

Bosnia-Herzegovina, winter 1992: *'Dido'* is Bosnian for 'grandfather' or 'old man'. 'Dido Group' served under the Ministry of the Interior, until it was disbanded and its personnel were absorbed by local commando units of I Corps of the Bosnia-Herzegovina Army (*Armija Republike Bosne i Hercegovine* – ARBiH). This photo, taken near Resnik south-west of Sarajevo, includes four British volunteers. (Private collection)

The Hague to stand trial before an International Criminal Tribunal for former Yugoslavia (ICTY). During this long-drawn-out process the Serbian leader and former President of Yugoslavia, Slobodan Milošević, was found dead in his cell on 11 March 2006. Radovan Karadzić, President of Republika Srpska (the Serb enclave within Bosnia-Herzegovina) evaded capture until 2008, but was sentenced in 2016 to 40 years' imprisonment (increased to life in 2019) for war crimes, crimes against humanity, and genocide. His commander-in-chief of the Bosnian-Serb Army (*Vojska Republike Srpske* – VRS), ColGen Ratko Mladić, was not captured until 2011; tried on the same charges in 2012, he was found guilty and sentenced to life imprisonment in 2017.

WAR IN THE 21st CENTURY

PRIVATE MILITARY COMPANIES

Governments routinely provide armed forces personnel as military instructors for 'friendly' nations. It was inevitable that enterprising individuals would realize that they could form commercial companies to supply the same services, and a lot more besides. Such a company would not necessarily be influenced by factors that might restrict governments. It could operate on behalf of commercial corporations with a vested interest in restoring order in a volatile region, and might also tender for contracts considered too sensitive for direct foreign government involvement.

Pioneers of military outsourcing

The forerunners of today's private military companies (PMCs) emerged during the Cold War. In September 1962, Egyptian troops invaded the Yemen to support a military coup against the ruling Imam. Egypt's President Nasser was backed by the Soviet Union; this represented a serious threat not only to the oilfields of Saudi Arabia but also to Britain's bases in Aden. An innovative solution was proposed by the founder of Britain's Special Air Service (SAS) in World War II , LtCol David Stirling, together with a friend, the Conservative government minister Julian Amery. With government approval, and financial support provided by the Saudis, Stirling called on wartime contacts and organized a private war in the Yemen, in which British mercenaries trained and led Royalist guerrillas in operations against the Republican forces supported by Egypt and the Soviet Union.

After a ceasefire in 1965, Stirling played a key role in winning for Britain a major defence deal with the Saudis. It was the beginning of the modern arms trade with the Middle East, and of an enduring business relationship between the United Kingdom and Saudi Arabia.

Stirling and another ex-SAS officer, John Woodhouse, formed WatchGuard International, an organization that would provide Middle Eastern and African leaders with British military professionals to protect their governments from violent insurrection. Also associated with retired British Army officers was KMS (an abbreviation of Keeni-Meeni Services, and a reference to SAS undercover operations in Aden). Founded in 1974, KMS would conduct military training primarily in Arab countries.

During Executive Outcomes' active assistance to the Angolan army in fighting UNITA in the early 1990s, a South African pilot with EO is photographed at Saurimo, inspecting a slightly damaged T-54/55 main battle tank. (Private collection)

Another British company, Gurkha Security Guards (GSG) Ltd, was formed in 1989. GSG attracted unwanted media attention after the deaths in Sierra Leone in February 1995 of two military 'advisers', Andy Myers from the UK and American Bob Mackenzie.

Pioneering American companies included the Vinnell Corporation, with a well-established subsidiary servicing the Saudi Arabian National Guard since 1975. Military Professional Resources Incorporated (MPRI) provided training for Croatian forces following their final successful offensive in western Krajina in August 1995, and has also been involved in Bosnia, Equatorial Guinea, Colombia, Iraq and Afghanistan.

Executive Outcomes

One PMC would have a significant impact on events in war-torn Africa. Its founder, Eeben Barlow, had joined the South African Defence Force in 1974. As an officer in the Engineer Corps, he was loaned in 1980 to 32 Bn's

Sierre Leone, 1990s; South African and Angolan contractors of Executive Outcomes on board an ex-Soviet helicopter. (Private collection)

Sierra Leone, mid-1990s: Fijian contractor Kauata 'Fred' Marafano. He had joined the British Army in 1961, passing SAS selection a few years later. In the mid-1980s, after 21 years in the SAS, he embarked on a career in the private security sector, and would spend years working in Sierra Leone. The helicopter is an ex-Soviet Mi-17, fondly referred to by its crew as 'Bokkie'. The pilot was South African Neall Ellis, and Marafano was the loadmaster/gunner. Just visible (left) is thought to be the armourer/technician Tilahun Kebede, from Ethiopia. Sandline offered the helicopter to Ellis and his team in lieu of cash payment on termination of contract. 'Bokkie' subsequently became the property of a new company, Jessair (in which Marafano and Ellis were partners), which would be contracted by the Economic Community of West African States Monitoring Group (ECOMOG) for logistics resupply to outlying bases. (Patrick Robert/Sygma via| Getty Images)

Reconnaissance Wing, where he remained until January 1983. He went on to serve in military intelligence, rising to the rank of major. In March 1989 Barlow resigned from the SADF as a prerequisite to joining the covert Civil Cooperation Bureau (CCB). As part of his cover, Executive Outcomes (EO) was registered in Pretoria as what was termed a 'close corporation'. Outwardly, EO provided training programmes for South African Special Forces, but its main purposes were to generate income for CCB operations and to act as a clearing house for such funds. When the CCB ceased to exist in mid-1990, Barlow returned to civilian life and continued to market EO as a specialist training company.

In early 1993 a meeting took place between Barlow and two Britons: ex-Scots Guards and SAS officer Simon Mann, and his business associate Tony Buckingham. Buckingham wished to retrieve valuable oil-drilling equipment from the northern Angolan coastal town of Soyo, then under UNITA control. Barlow agreed to provide personnel to safeguard the recovery operation, once Soyo had been seized by the Angolan Armed Forces (*Forças Armadas de Angolanas* – FAA).

Recruiting from among former members of the SADF, Barlow was able to put 72 men on the ground by March 1993. The force was transported by helicopter as part of an assault in conjunction with FAA troops, who were to arrive by sea. Quefiquena, south-west of Soyo, was selected as the first objective. Executive Outcomes was engaged in some of the heaviest fighting yet seen in northern Angola, and two months later had succeeded in its mission, at the cost of three men killed and several wounded. Barlow's company was on its way to becoming a major player in a new world where enterprising individuals could win multi-million-dollar contracts – circumventing protracted political negotiations, and expediting matters by taking prompt and effective military action.

As a result of the Soyo operation, EO was contracted by the Angolan government to assist the FAA in its ongoing campaign against UNITA. Veterans of South Africa's border war were now battling their erstwhile allies on behalf of a former enemy. By all accounts they did so with undiminished enthusiasm, leading to a ceasefire on 22 November 1994 (fighting would resume in mid-1997). By the end of its nearly two and a half years in Angola, EO had fielded some 500 operators, and was as much a true mercenary force as Mike Hoare's 5 Commando had been in the Congo three decades earlier.

By the time the Angola operation ended in January 1996, Barlow had already been contracted by Capt Valentine Strasser, leader of Sierra Leone's National Provisional Ruling Council. EO was tasked with ending a rebellion by the Revolutionary United Front (RUF) subsequent to the involvement earlier in the year of Gurkha Security Guards Ltd. Between May 1995 and February 1997 EO succeeded in halting the RUF advance on the capital, Freetown, and was instrumental in securing important economic and strategic

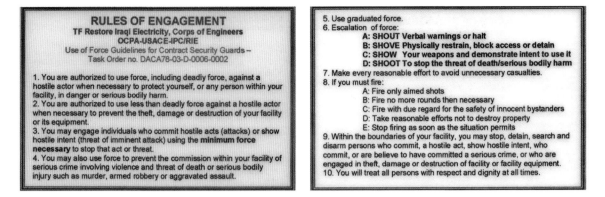

RULES OF ENGAGEMENT
TF Restore Iraqi Electricity, Corps of Engineers
OCPA-USACE-IPC/RIE
Use of Force Guidelines for Contract Security Guards –
Task Order no. DACA78-03-D-0006-0002

1. You are authorized to use force, including deadly force, against a hostile actor when necessary to protect yourself, or any person within your facility, in danger or serious bodily harm.
2. You are authorized to use less than deadly force against a hostile actor when necessary to prevent the theft, damage or destruction of your facility or its equipment.
3. You may engage individuals who commit hostile acts (attacks) or show hostile intent (threat of imminent attack) using the **minimum force necessary** to stop that act or threat.
4. You may also use force to prevent the commission within your facility of serious crime involving violence and threat of death or serious bodily injury such as murder, armed robbery or aggravated assault.

5. Use graduated force.
6. Escalation of force:
    A: SHOUT Verbal warnings or halt
    B: SHOVE Physically restrain, block access or detain
    C: SHOW Your weapons and demonstrate intent to use it
    D: SHOOT To stop the threat of death/serious bodily harm
7. Make every reasonable effort to avoid unnecessary casualties.
8. If you must fire:
    A: Fire only aimed shots
    B: Fire no more rounds then necessary
    C: Fire with due regard for the safety of innocent bystanders
    D: Take reasonable efforts not to destroy property
    E: Stop firing as soon as the situation permits
9. Within the boundaries of your facility, you may stop, detain, search and disarm persons who commit, a hostile act, show hostile intent, who commit, or are believe to have committed a serious crime, or who are engaged in theft, damage or destruction of facility or facility equipment.
10. You will treat all persons with respect and dignity at all times.

assets, including the diamond-mining region of Kono in the eastern province. Notwithstanding the United Nations Mercenary Convention (broadly similar to that of Geneva), EO also provided protection for aid convoys of the UN's World Food Programme.

Eeben Barlow resigned as director of EO in June 1997, and the company he had established ceased trading 18 months later. In 2009 Barlow was appointed chairman of another PMC, named Specialised Tasks, Training, Equipment and Protection International. STTEPI was reported in 2015 to be in northern Nigeria providing training for local forces combating Boko Haram.

Early Rules of Engagement card for private military company contractors in Iraq. (Private collection)

Sandline International
In 1997, EO was linked with Sandline International, a PMC which had been contracted by the Papua New Guinea government to assist in its operations against rebel forces on the island of Bougainville in the Solomons. This did not sit well with PNG Defence Force BrigGen Jerry Singirok. In mid-March, Tim Spicer, a former lieutenant-colonel in the Scots Guards and a key figure in Sandline, was detained together with two South African EO representatives and some 40 contractors. Singirok was promptly dismissed as military commander by Prime Minister Sir Julias Chan. Rioting followed, and amid the furore Chan was forced to resign. All detainees were released shortly afterwards. In spite of its abortive nature, the Bougainville operation was a financial success for Sandline: following legal action, the company reportedly received a pay-out of more than $13 million.

Iraq, summer 2005: a personal security detail (PSD) with their Toyota Landcruisers at the main vehicle park in Baghdad's Green Zone. Left to right: the author; Riaan de Beer (South African); Des Cobban (Rhodesian); Mattias Englund (Swedish); two local nationals; and Craig Gomm (South African). (Des Cobban collection)

It was not long before Spicer was back in the news. In Sierra Leone on 25 May 1997, President Ahmad Tejan Kabbah was overthrown in a coup orchestrated by Maj Johnny Paul Koroma. The following year, the so-called 'arms-to-Africa' affair saw Sandline accused of breaching UN Security Council Resolution 1132 by supplying arms and ammunition to Sierra Leone for use by anti-government forces with the intention of reinstating Kabbah. In the event, Kabbah was restored to power with the assistance

Iraq, 2005: view from the rear armoured SUV during a PSD high-profile road move to Baghdad International Airport. The airport road, known as 'Route Irish', was rightly considered to be among the most dangerous in the world at that time. Scarring on the road is evidence of previous incidents involving vehicle-borne improvised explosive devices (VBIEDs). Civilian traffic can be seen maintaining a healthy distance so as to avoid getting caught up in any violent incidents. (Des Cobban)

of Nigerian forces. Spicer and Sandline were investigated, but the matter was dropped following suggestions of British Foreign and Commonwealth Office involvement.

The 'Wonga coup': Equatorial Guinea, 2004

In March 2004, Spicer's associate Simon Mann was at Zimbabwe's Harare International Airport to meet a private Boeing 727. On board were nearly 70 mercenaries, more than half of them black Africans. They had expected to collect weapons and ammunition before proceeding to Equatorial Guinea to overthrow President Teodoro Obiang Nguema. However, authorities in both Equatorial Guinea and Zimbabwe had been tipped off (by whom, and for what motive, was the subject of murky speculation).

Mann and two colleagues, along with the airliner's passengers and crew, were arrested. A day or two later 15 men, including ex-EO commander S.N. 'Nick' du Toit, were seized in Equatorial Guinea. Among others implicated in the affair was Mark Thatcher, the South Africa-resident son of former British Prime Minister Margaret Thatcher. He was accused of helping to fund a plot to oust President Obiang, a charge he denied (he would escape with a hefty fine and a suspended sentence).

Of those apprehended, most were allowed to return to South Africa, where they were charged under the country's 1998 Regulation of Foreign Military Assistance Act; the case was thrown out, and all were released. In contrast, in Zimbabwe Simon Mann was tried for weapons offences, found guilty, and handed a 7-year (reduced to 4-year) custodial sentence. In Equatorial Guinea, the even less fortunate du Toit was sentenced to 34 years' imprisonment.

At the end of January 2008, the Zimbabwean authorities extradited Mann to Equatorial Guinea, where he was informed that he would spend 34 years and four months in prison. Few expected that any of the mercenaries would survive their incarceration. Bur in November 2009, Mann and the remaining four conspirators (another had died in custody) were granted a

Mosul, Iraq, 2004–05: this group reflects the very cosmopolitan make-up of PSD teams at the time. (Kneeling left) is American Eugene Pomeroy – ex-US Army and Rhodesian SAS; (kneeling centre, hatless) is Paul French from the UK – ex-21 SAS, Rhodesian SAS and Selous Scouts (see Plate B3), and SADF Recce Commandos; (kneeling right) are two Fijians; and the contractors manning the truck-mounted machine guns are both from Nepal. (Paul French)

pardon on humanitarian grounds by President Obiang. They were released the following day.

IRAQ AND AFGHANISTAN

On 11 September 2001, two hijacked airliners were flown into New York City's World Trade Center. This, the world's worst terrorist attack, prompted US President George W. Bush to declare his commitment to pursuing the perpetrators. As the so-called 'War on Terror' intensified, so too did the demand for former servicemen and women whose skills could be utilized for high-risk ventures in hostile environments. During the early years of the 21st century, PMCs reliant on ex-military professionals became heavily involved alongside national military forces.

Iraq and Afghanistan provided ample opportunities for the security industry. PMCs offered a range of services, including risk assessment and management, close protection, and awareness training. Clients included government departments, business corporations, and non-governmental organizations (NGOs). Prominent among major American security providers were Blackwater USA, DynCorp International and Triple Canopy Incorporated. British companies included Control Risks Group (CRG), ArmorGroup International plc, Erinys International Ltd, and Aegis Defence Services Limited.

The second Gulf War, Operation 'Iraqi Freedom', began on 20 March 2003 ostensibly as a continuation of the War on Terror. The large international coalition that had liberated Kuwait from Iraqi President Saddam Hussein's invasion in the first Gulf War of 1990-91 could not be rebuilt, but President Bush enjoyed the cooperation of Britain's Prime Minister Tony Blair. This more limited Coalition's stated objective was to

Insurgents would regularly rocket Iraq's Basra International Airport, where security companies and their clients were accommodated in a number of compounds. Here, a security contractor (right) and a client await the 'all clear' in a bomb shelter during a night-time alert. (Private collection)

Bashiqa, northern Iraq, 2017: security contractor Alan Boydell (right) with a Canadian colleague. They were part of a group tasked with the safety of a civilian EOD team following up on the Kurdish advance against Daesh. Compared to the early days in Iraq they are well equipped, with modified East German AKs and personalized tactical equipment. (Private collection)

overthrow Saddam Hussein's regime and to rid the world of any threat posed by Iraq's alleged weapons of mass destruction (WMDs). On 1 May 2003, after the occupation of Baghdad, Bush declared an end to major combat operations – a declaration soon revealed as somewhat premature.

No WMDs had been found. Saddam went into hiding; he was eventually captured, subjected to a show trial by an Iraqi court, and executed. He had been a ruthless tyrant, but he had proved able to control a diverse nation. By disbanding his army and security apparatus with no realistic plan as to how to replace them, the United States had unleashed chaos among the divided and well-armed peoples of a failed state.

In the wake of the invasion, Ambassador L. Paul Bremer, a career diplomat, was appointed to head the Coalition Provisional Authority (CPA). Reporting to US Defense Secretary Donald Rumsfeld, the CPA comprised American and British officials responsible for coordinating the occupation administration's efforts to restore law and order and essential services. Contracts for reconstruction projects were awarded by the US Agency for International Development (USAID), and for oil sector reconstruction by the US Army Corps of Engineers. All major contracts went to US companies, which, in turn, sub-contracted to mainly American, British and Australian firms – whose safety in-country was reliant on PMC security providers.

The British PMC Aegis Defence Services Ltd had been established in 2002 by Sandline associate Tim Spicer. In June 2004 Aegis successfully applied for a $293 million US government tender to provide core reconstruction security support services in Iraq. The American company DynCorp formally objected to the US Congress, citing Spicer's controversial past, but to no avail. By mid-2007 Aegis fielded some 1,200 men and women at locations throughout Iraq, making it one of the most powerful security providers in the country.

Security providers charged the client a hefty fee for each contractor, who was, in turn, paid a day rate of several hundred US dollars. But in order to secure contracts, it was often necessary for companies to undercut competitors. One of the first British security companies to arrive in Iraq protected its potential profits by introducing a substantial reduction in contractor day rates; this provoked resignations, which, in turn, created a manpower deficit. This was remedied by recruiting nationalities for whom the reduced rate was still a considerable sum. Other companies were quick to follow this trend.

In the beginning, companies could afford to be selective in choosing contractors, but there was, after all, only a limited number of ex-special forces applicants available. For British PMCs, former members of the Parachute Regiment and Royal Marines Commandos were the preferred choice, but in reality anybody with a solid military background stood an equal chance. Less scrupulous employers took whomever they could. One applicant whose military service did not extend beyond basic training was told at his interview that the company was mainly concerned with 'putting bums on seats' – i.e. numbers, rather than quality. For the security provider, hiring inexperienced personnel equated to money in the bank, but it jeopardized the lives of contractors trying to cope in an often difficult and very dangerous environment.

In 2003, it was not unheard of for those newly-arrived in Iraq to be deployed without precise instructions regarding their role, and with minimal and substandard equipment. For stand-alone teams it could be especially challenging, and personnel relied on their own ingenuity and improvisation. Accommodation and vehicles were rented locally, and fuel usually had to be purchased on the black market. Iraqi arms dealers were paid to supplement or replace faulty weapons and ammunition. Typically, no maps would be provided of the area of operations, and there was no such thing as daily situation reports unless these could be acquired from cooperative Coalition forces.

It was not long before security providers became better organized, leading to improved conditions for contractors. At the same time, however, Iraqis were becoming impatient with the practically lawless conditions and the apparent lack of progress in repairing their country's ruined infrastructure. On 31 March 2004, five US Army soldiers were killed by a roadside bomb at Habbaniyah. At nearby Fallujah, four Blackwater security contractors were shot dead. Their vehicles were set on fire – with them inside – and afterwards the charred corpses were strung up from a bridge over the Euphrates. This ended any speculation as to what contractors could expect if seized by hostile locals. These two events also set in motion the first of two major operations by Coalition forces to pacify Fallujah.

By spring 2005 insurgents had modified their tactics, and were deliberately targeting security teams. Those travelling to and from Baghdad International Airport on so-called 'Route Irish' were especially at risk. This was highlighted in April 2005, when one man was shot and killed and two were wounded when a supposedly low-profile personal security detail (PSD) from Edinburgh Risk & Security Management was ambushed. Team members had compromised themselves by adopting an overly aggressive posture. A video of what followed was posted online. What is not generally known is that a low-profile PSD from another company was also present. That team maintained their cover, and escaped the killing zone with only minor damage from stray rounds. The team leader later observed that in his experience there were those who knew how to operate in the low-profile role, and others who were quite unable to grasp the concept.

On 16 September 2007, 17 Iraqis were killed and many wounded when Blackwater contractors opened fire while in congested traffic in Baghdad. According to Blackwater, its men were acting in self-defence; according to Iraqi eyewitnesses, they fired indiscriminately. Blackwater was already known for its aggressive tactics in Iraq, but these latest killings would do irreparable harm to the reputation of Blackwater in particular and all security providers in general. (In an effort to reinvent itself, Blackwater USA was

Security contractors also operated in Afghanistan. For low-profile tasks they often travelled in unarmoured vehicles and worked together with 'local nationals'. Gordon Brindley (right, in local costume) spent several years in Afghanistan. Previously he had served in the British and Rhodesian armies, and in South Africa in Pathfinder Company, 44 Para Brigade. Subsequently, he was involved in the first abortive mission with Peter McAleese to target FARC in Colombia. (Gordon Brindley)

Seen at FOB Shaft, a former Soviet air base at Shindand, in Herat Province, Afghanistan. (Private collection)

rebranded as Blackwater Worldwide, then as Xe Services LLC, and in December 2011 as Academi.)

In January 2009 Barack Obama succeeded George W. Bush as President of the United States, and thereafter the all but unwinnable and increasingly unpopular war in Iraq became secondary to operations in Afghanistan. American forces were scheduled to be withdrawn from Iraq by the end of 2012.

In the meantime, NATO's International Security Assistance Force (ISAF) in the mountains and river valleys of Afghanistan continued to fight the 'War on Terror', while aid agencies channelled millions of dollars to fund local projects. These included road construction, the ultimate aim of which was to facilitate access for companies eager to exploit the country's largely untapped natural resources. With diminishing prospects for Western security providers in Iraq, the focus shifted to Afghanistan.

Today, two decades into the 21st century, security contractors continue to operate in hostile environments – not only on land, but also at sea in an anti-piracy role.

DEALING WITH THE FALL-OUT

Daesh

One of the consequences of the 2003 US-led invasion of Iraq and the subsequent collapse of law and order was the rise of Salafi (Sunni) and, to a lesser degree, Shia Islamic fundamentalism. Among those to achieve notoriety during this time was a Jordanian Al Qaeda *jihadi* leader, Abu Musab al-Zarqawi. Taking advantage of sectarian tensions, he acquired followers and support for 'al-Qaeda in Iraq' (AQI). Zarqawi was killed in an

---

H AFGHANISTAN & SYRIA

(1) 'Happy Hem', security contractor; Afghanistan, 2009
As second-in-command of a personal security detail (PSD), 'Happy Hem' played an essential role in safeguarding expatriate engineers during a road construction project in Badakhshan Province, north-east Afghanistan. Hem was one of two Nepalese ex-soldiers with the group, who were always professional, uncomplaining, and, importantly, also spoke the local dialect. Hem's uniform is a company-issue royal-blue baseball cap and polo shirt both displaying the company logo, cargo trousers and desert boots. His issue tactical vest is not of the best quality, but sufficient for the task. A Motorola radio is carried for communicating with the rest of the team. The AK is locally sourced, and probably a leftover from the Soviet occupation of Afghanistan.

(2) 'Local national' security contractor; Afghanistan, 2009
Private military/security companies provide 'LNs' with employment in a variety of roles, including in administration, as translators, but also as PSD team members. This Afghan, trained and paid by a British company, is fairly typical of those who operate in more remote regions (the figure is a composite of two comrades who were photographed together). His

rifle is the ubiquitous AK, in this case personalized by the decorations painted on the buttstock and magazine. The cap, tactical vest and desert boots are part of his company kit issue. Training was the responsibility of PSD team leaders and their 2 i/cs.

(3): 'Fran', Kurdish People's Defence Units; Syria, 2016
More than 20 years after leaving the Frankopan Bn in Bosnia in August 1992, Fran would join other foreign volunteers in the Kurdish *Yekîneyên Parastina Gel* (YPG), fighting against *Daesh* (ISIS) in Syria. The digital camouflage-pattern uniform seen here was manufactured by Kurdish tailors with material from China, but resembles USMC 'Marpat'; the contrasting field cap is Syrian Army issue. The hardly-visible slung rifle is a Chinese folding-stock AK, and the web equipment is a mixture of miscellaneous items. Draped over his right shoulder is a *keffiyeh* or *shemagh* in shades of brown. On his left yoke harness is a Russian AK bayonet (in Fran's opinion, 'more a tool than a weapon; it is a big knife very useful to open metal ammo boxes.') His smooth-soled boots are American, 'the best desert boots I have ever had', and his sunglasses are ESS ballistic.

The author in northern Afghanistan. This photo was taken during a mobile task lasting several days and covering more than 840 miles (1,350km). Equipment included a Blackhawk tactical vest, Motorola radio, 9mm Glock handgun and folding-stock AK. (Private collection)

American airstrike in 2006, but, under a succession of leaders, his doctrine would influence the emergence of other extremist organizations. After his death, AQI merged with other groups to form the 'Islamic State in Iraq' (ISI). From 2007 American forces managed to suppress ISI, but it re-emerged a few years later.

In 2011, disenchantment in the Arab world led to widespread anti-government protests – the so-called 'Arab Spring'. In early 2013 the then-leader of ISI, Abu Bakr al-Baghdadi, relocated to Syria. ISI became known as the 'Islamic State of Iraq and Syria' (ISIS – or *Daesh*, the derogatory Arabic acronym preferred by opposing groups). In mid-2014, al-Baghdadi announced the creation of a caliphate – a Muslim theocratic state – extending from Aleppo in Syria to Diyala in Iraq. Daesh would quickly earn a reputation for extreme violence and brutality, encouraging the use of torture, rape and mass murder, and relying on social media to spread its doctrine. Daesh actions in Iraq and Syria inspired Islamic extremists worldwide, and the ranks of Daesh fighters were filled with thousands of foreign volunteers, among them Western converts.

Daesh would eventually be worn down, first during battles in Iraq and then in Syria, where its militants had taken part in the civil war against President Bashar al-Assad's government as part of their efforts to expand the caliphate. In late 2014 Daesh began an assault on Kobane, and a US-led multinational force responded by carrying out air strikes. On the ground, Daesh was opposed by various fighting forces, notably the Kurdish People's Defence Units (*Yekîneyên Parastina Gel* – YPG), formed by the large and thriving Kurdish ethnic community in the region. In 2015 the YPG formed an alliance with the moderate anti-Assad Syrian Democratic Forces (SDF), which were favoured by the US-led Coalition.

By spring 2019 the YPG, aided and assisted by the United States, and together with the SDF, had defeated Daesh. But the YPG's association with the Kurdistan Worker's Party (*Partiya Karkerên Kurdistanê* – PKK), considered by Turkey to be a terrorist organization, would lead to a *volte face* by the Trump administration. Unopposed by the US government, Turkey's President Recep Tayyip Erdoğan launched a major military operation in October 2019 with the aim of creating a buffer zone along Turkey's southern border inside northern Syria, expelling both the YPG and SDF. The Kurds, who had undertaken much of the fighting against Daesh, were thus betrayed.

Among those who fought within the ranks of the YPG against Daesh were a number of Westerners, including 'Fran', the French former paratrooper who had served with Croatian forces during the 1990s war in Yugoslavia. In 2015 he joined the YPG, remaining for six months and participating in mobile actions, negotiating the flat terrain in Toyota 'technicals' and, with American air support, helping to seize Daesh-held areas. The following year he returned for a further eight months, but due to a training injury was unable to take part in the Minbic (Manbij) offensive, during which Daesh was eradicated from that city and its surrounding area.

In 2017, Fran's *Tabûr* (roughly equivalent to a platoon) was airlifted in an American Bell-Boeing V-22 Osprey to take part in the capture of Tabqa. There he was seriously wounded by machine-gun fire; he was casevaced by

Standing guard: one of the many LNs hired by a British PMC for an expatriate-led security force in eastern Afghanistan. Compare with Plate H2. As a result of the Taliban take-over of much of the country in August 2021, and potential repercussions against those connected with Western companies, this man's identity has been obscured. (Private collection)

Toyota to the Euphrates and ferried across the river by dinghy, before finding himself in a US military field hospital. After surgery, he spent two months recovering at Minbic before rejoining his unit and subsequently crewing heavy weapons. Fran would see further action during the fighting for Rakka, where another French volunteer was shot dead beside him during house-clearing. In all, Fran spent 24 months with the YPG. By the time he departed from Rojava in December 2017, Daesh – which had once controlled about 30 per cent of Syria and 40 per cent of Iraq – had lost 95 per cent of its territory.

Wagner

The West is not alone in making good use of PMCs: consider the secretive Russian-based Wagner Group. It has been speculated that this shadowy organization was created by Yevgeny Prighozin, a Russian oligarch on close terms with President Vladimir Putin. With no official ties to his government, it provides plausible deniability. Toward the end of 2015 Wagner was reported to be operating in Syria in support of President Assad, and was involved in freeing Palmyra on two occasions – in March 2016 and again in 2017.

In Africa, Wagner appears to have stepped into the vacuum left by Executive Outcomes. It operated in Sudan in 2018–19 on behalf of the government, and subsequently conducted training for the Central African Republic's Armed Forces (*Forces armées centrafricaines* – FACA). For several months during 2019–20 Wagner contractors were in Mozambique,

In Afghanistan, PMCs routinely took on roles previously the responsibility of NATO forces, thus freeing military personnel for other tasks. At FOB Shaft, an ISAF Italian mobile patrol departs, watched by an Afghan security guard (left) trained and supervised by British ex-Royal Marines. (Private collection)

Northern Syria, 2015: French volunteer 'Fran' (seated, front centre) with some members of a Kurdish YPG *Tabûr* just before the Frenchman's first departure from Syria (he would return in 2016 – see Plate H3). This mobile light infantry platoon totalled 29 male and 10 female fighters. The three women (far right) had all been wounded in action, suffering facial wounds from grenade and RPG fragments, and in one case from a bullet through the mouth which, incredibly, missed her tongue and teeth. The central man standing alone behind the group had lost a leg. To the left of him, wearing a green sweater, is 'Berodan', who lost his life in 2017. Next to him is 'Bower', a close friend of Fran's, who gave the Frenchman the *nom de guerre* 'Baba Sidar', and who would be killed by a mine or IED. The man sitting at far left would be seriously wounded near Shedade.

Fran explained: 'The moment was quite emotional. I was leaving, going home and back to the World, but those teens were staying. For them, no way out. Many of the boys will be killed, crippled, or will lose a limb. And the girls will stay virgin and will never bear children.' (Private collection)

although whether to conduct operations against Islamist extremists or to provide security for President Filipe Nyusi (or both) is unclear. In any event, by March 2020 Wagner had withdrawn from Mozambique, where air support was then being provided by helicopters and fixed-wing aircraft crewed by contractors of the South African-based Dyck Advisory Group (DAG).

Elsewhere in Africa, Wagner remained active. In Libya in 2020 it was reportedly assisting rebel forces against the internationally recognized Government of National Accord (GNA) in Tripoli and its Turkish-backed Syrian fighters.

Conclusion

It is not within the scope of this work to dwell on the motivation of the countless Muslims who flocked to join Daesh in Iraq and Syria, but one can understand why so many volunteers went to the Middle East to oppose them. Some were adventurers, but many were idealists. Most considered their chosen cause, quite simply, as one of good versus evil. Is there a word to describe such men – and women?

It is not only in the Middle East where foreign volunteers may be attracted to fight in a war where ethnicity and/or religion are key factors. Consider, for instance, the break-up of Yugoslavia, where few, if any, could expect to profit financially.

The Rhodesian recruiting brochure *This is The Army* made it clear that: 'With our emphasis on motivated manpower, mercenaries are not, and never have been, employed by the Rhodesian Army'. Those foreigners who served in Rhodesia, and later in the South African Defence Force, had more in common with the Gurkhas in the British Army, the different nationalities in the French Foreign Legion, and the few foreigners in the Spanish Legion.

Those who do seek their fortune by involvement in other people's wars fall into a different category. As we have seen, mercenaries were especially active in the second half of the 20th century. More recently, and particularly in Iraq and Afghanistan, the privatization of war has flourished as an immensely lucrative industry. Where there is war, there are likely to be private military companies. These corporations are, by definition, mercenary; but whether individual PMC contractors are mercenaries is largely a matter of perception.

SELECT BIBLIOGRAPHY

Barlow, Eeben, *Executive Outcomes: Against All Odds* (Galago Publishing (1999) Pty Ltd; 2007)

Burchett, Wilfred & Derek Roebuck, *The Whores of War: Mercenaries Today* (Penguin Books Ltd; 1977)

Dempster, Chris & Dave Tomkins, with Michel Parry, *Fire Power* (Corgi Books; 1978)

Gillmore, Graham, *Pathfinder Company: The Philistines* (30° South Pty Ltd; 2010)

Hoare, Mike, *Mercenary* (Robert Hale Ltd; 1967)

Hoare, Mike, *The Seychelles Affair* (Bantam Press; 1986)

Mann, Simon, *Cry Havoc* (John Blake Publishing Ltd; 2011)

McAleese, Peter, with Mark Bles, *No Mean Soldier: The Autobiography of a Professional Fighting Man* (Orion; 1993)

Mockler, Anthony, *The New Mercenaries: The History of the Mercenary from the Congo to the Seychelles* (Sidgwick & Jackson Ltd; 1985)

Pelton, Robert Young, *Licensed to Kill: Hired Guns in the War on Terror* (Crown Publishers; 2006)

Puren, Col Jerry, as told to Brian Pottinger, *Mercenary Commander* (Galago Publishing Pty Ltd; 1986)

Rogers, Anthony, *Someone Else's War; Mercenaries from 1960 to the Present* (HarperCollins Publishers; 1998)

Scahill, Jeremy, *Blackwater: The Rise of the World's Most Powerful Mercenary Army* (Nation Books; 2007)

Steiner, Rolf, with Yves-Guy Berges, *The Last Adventurer* (Little, Brown & Company; 1978)

Thomas, Neil, *The Odd-Job Man: No Time To Die* (Austin Macauley Publishers Ltd; 2021)

Tomkins, David, *Dirty Combat: Secret Wars and Serious Misadventures* (Mainstream Publishing Company (Edinburgh) Ltd; 2008)

Weinberg, Samantha, *Last of the Pirates: The Search for Bob Denard* (Jonathan Cape; 1994)

Periodicals, *passim:*

Combat and Survival (originally Aerospace Publishing, UK)

Raids (Histoire et Collections, Paris)

Soldier of Fortune (Omega Group Limited/ Soldier of Fortune Magazine, USA)

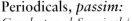

Deir-el-Zor front, Syria, November 2017: 'Fran' (right) as part of the crew of a Toyota Land Cruiser 'technical' mounting 14.5mm twin HMGs. After returning to Syria for the third and last time in 2017, he served with a *Tabûr* involved with US forces in reclaiming from Daesh the area of Tabqa. In this action Fran was struck by machine-gun fire, suffering a perforated lung and two broken ribs. After two months in hospital he rejoined his unit, subsequently serving heavy weapons, before finally departing in December 2017. Fran's webbing was probably captured from Daesh; the combat jacket is Turkish, of a type widely worn by YPG fighters; his shirt and trousers are American (found at Tabqa), and the cap is Syrian Army. The Toyota driver is an American, and the third man is from Germany (Private collection)

INDEX